DAVID AUSTIN'S
ENGLISH ROSES

DAVID AUSTIN'S
ENGLISH ROSES

DAVID AUSTIN

GARDEN·ART·PRESS

© 2012 David Austin
World copyright reserved

ISBN: 978 1 870673 70 9

(Parts of this text originally appeared in *Old Roses & English Roses* by David Austin, 1993 and *The Rose* by David Austin, 2009)

British Library Cataloguing-in-Publication Data:
A catalogue record for this book is available from the British Library

Printed in China for Garden Art Press, an imprint of the Antique Collectors' Club Ltd., Woodbridge, Suffolk IP12 4SD

CONTENTS

INTRODUCTION

This book is dedicated to my English Roses which originated from crosses made between selected Old Roses and Modern Hybrid Teas and Floribundas, and which first gained prominence in the 1970s. The result was a new type of rose that combines the delicate charm and fragrance of the Old Roses with the desirable wide colour range and excellent repeat-flowering abilities of the Modern Rose—and which is happily very disease resistant. They are, in fact, the new 'Old Roses', if I may be forgiven for the apparent contradiction in terms.

The principal aim in the breeding of English Roses has been to emphasise above anything else the beauty and fragrance of the individual flowers. As with Old Roses, these may be cup-shaped or in the form of a rosette, and nearly all of them exude a strong and delicious fragrance. Ranging from the beautiful Old Rose fragrance to the Tea Rose and Musk Rose fragrances with myrrh and many different fruits in between, no other roses can rival them in this respect.

Their growth is naturally graceful and shrubby, and this makes English Roses suitable for many different spots in the garden, although position is of course an issue with all roses, with north-facing sites often being unsuitable. Some form substantial shrubs 1.2 - 1.5m/4-5ft high where as others may be quite short, some have rounded bushy growth and others are gracefully arching or even upright. A number of the taller varieties can reach a height of about 2.5m/8 ft and make excellent repeat-flowering climbers. Others make excellent hedges or can be grown in large containers for the patio and balcony.

This versatility is one of the things that has contributed to the popularity of English Roses, and I would like to make a plea for them to be planted in groups of three or more of one variety where space allows. These should be so close that they gradually grow together to form what is, to all intents and purposes, one shrub. Planted singly roses can look a little insubstantial, a group planting however affords much better visual impact with a bushier whole and more assured continuous flowering, since when one plant has temporarily ceased to flower the others may take over.

In dedicated rose borders, the soft colours of the English Roses mix admirably with those of Old and Shrub roses, and have the benefit of providing a mass of blooms when the flowering period of the latter has already finished. Pinks, blush pinks, lilacs, purples, reds, yellows, whites, creams, apricots and copper-coloured varieties are all represented. English Roses also mix well with other plants and are very at home in a mixed border but, as with all recurrent-flowering roses, cannot withstand too much competition, so it is necessary to keep them at a reasonable distance from other strong-growing plants.

In this book I include all the most noteworthy of my English Roses; but the work does not stop and we continue to breed new varieties (five were added to the collection this year). Companion volumes in the series will cover the forerunner to English Roses, the Old Roses; also the numerous and very beautiful Climbing and Rambling Roses.

THE ENGLISH ROSES

The story of the rose does not end. It follows the course of history, evolving as it goes—taking on new forms, new colours and new habits of growth and foliage. Consider for example the beautiful old European roses with their wonderful fragrance, some of which themselves had parents with their origins in the Middle East—the Gallicas, the Damasks, the Centifolias, the Moss Roses and the Albas. Also the China Roses, which flower throughout the summer, and how, in time, the ability to repeat flower passed to the Portland Roses, the Bourbons and the Hybrid Perpetuals, which had much of the same beauty as the Old Roses. These eventually gave way to the Hybrid Teas with their elegant buds and often bright colours. Later, their place was shared by their close relations, the Floribundas. During

A garden of English Roses at David Austin Rose Nurseries. **Perdita** *is at the front; the yellow rose is* **Graham Thomas**

this time, roses have been developed as climbers, as shrubs, small bushes and tiny miniatures. They have taken on many forms and colours: which begs the question, what is there left to do?

Many fine representatives of all these roses—old and new—are thankfully still with us; they continue to be grown in our gardens. I think that there is still much that can and should be done. This largely concerns the actual beauty of the rose. There was a tendency among plant breeders to assume that however they manipulate it genetically for colour, size, floriferousness, disease-resistance and so on, the resulting rose will inevitably retain its beauty. Unfortunately, this is not always so and some of the roses of today have declined in beauty—and often in fragrance, too—when compared with those of the past.

Francine Austin. A dainty Noisette hybrid, with the long, wiry stems, nicely spaced flowers and sheeny petals of its parent. A small shrub with elegant, arching growth

THE DEVELOPMENT OF THE ENGLISH ROSES

Back in the late 1940s it occurred to me that it would be beneficial to combine the beauty of the Old Roses with the practical virtues of Modern Roses in one range of roses. It seemed to me that the form of flower of the Old Roses was the ideal shape for a rose, rather than the long buds of the Hybrid Tea—beautiful though these may sometimes be. Most importantly, the Old Rose shape offers a much wider range of form and beauty: the single or semi-double bloom with its delicate beauty; the flat rosette; the cupped rosette and the recurved rosette. We also have deeply cupped flowers and these may be open with exposed stamens or filled with small petals. Even these categories can vary enormously between one variety and another—but also according to the stage of the bloom: first of all as a bud; later, the partly open flower; and finally the fully open flowers—each stage offering a new type of beauty. The Hybrid Tea flower, on the other hand, is only beautiful in the bud which is, of necessity, short-lived.

Similarly, the shrubby growth of the Old Roses is not only more useful in the garden—being more suitable for mingling with other plants in the border—but is also more beautiful in itself and very importantly, is capable of displaying its flowers to much greater effect and in a variety of different ways. A bloom becomes even finer when seen on a well-formed shrub.

At the same time, the Modern Roses have their advantages. Unlike the Old Roses, they flower throughout the summer and have a much wider range of colour. The colours of the Old Roses are confined to white through pink to crimson and purple shades, whereas the Modern Roses have numerous shades of yellow, flame, apricot, peach and so on.

When I took my first tentative steps to combine the virtues of the roses of the past with those of the present day, I was simply an amateur breeder, but over the last fifty years or so I have devoted my time to the development of what I have chosen to call 'English Roses'. While putting the very complex qualities of beauty and fragrance before all others, at the same time we have tried to encourage beauty and elegance of growth and foliage. Only after these come the very important qualities of disease-resistance, freedom of flowering, hardiness and so on for, essential as these characteristics are, a rose is of little value if it is not beautiful.

The earliest English Roses were nearly always the result of crossing old Gallica Roses with Floribundas and sometimes with Modern Hybrid Teas. Some of my very first hybrids were between the Floribunda 'Dainty Maid' and a Gallica Rose called 'Belle Isis'. The most important result of this cross was the still widely-grown 'Constance Spry', which has magnificent, large, deeply cupped flowers of a lovely shade of rich pink. It was first introduced as a shrub, in which form it easily reaches 2.5m / 8ft in height and as much across, often more. Only later did we find that it is even better when grown as a climber. This rose was an immediate success, even though it was only summer flowering.

The rose 'Belle Isis' was, in fact, a short shrub and 'Dainty Maid' was a strong

but not very tall Floribunda of excellent constitution and health. Graham Thomas pointed out to me that 'Constance Spry' has a myrrh fragrance, which is very rare among garden roses. He thought that 'Belle Isis' must, itself, have originally been the result of a chance cross between the Ayrshire Rose 'Splendens' and a Centifolia, as 'Splendens' was the only rose he knew that also had a myrrh scent. This would suggest that 'Belle Isis' was not a pure Gallica, in spite of the fact that it had always been regarded as such, and explained the excellent climbing properties of 'Constance Spry'. In any case, 'Constance Spry' was responsible for bringing the lovely myrrh fragrance to English Roses.

'Constance Spry' was then itself back-crossed with other Floribundas and

***Lilian Austin** is less of an Old Rose than most English Roses, but it is an ideal shrub for the border*

11

Hybrid Teas and these gradually brought repeat-flowering to the first English Roses, which included 'Canterbury', 'Dame Prudence', 'The Miller', 'The Prioress', 'The Yeoman' and 'Wife of Bath', names all taken from Chaucer's *The Canterbury Tales*.

In an attempt to bring dark crimson to our roses, I used the Floribunda 'Dusky Maiden' and crossed this with the beautiful Old Gallica 'Tuscany Superb'. As with 'Constance Spry', the result was a large shrub but with lovely deep crimson, rosette-shaped flowers and a wonderful Old Rose fragrance. I called this rose 'Chianti'. However, unlike 'Constance Spry', it formed a large but neat shrub. Again, we had the problem that 'Chianti' was only early-summer flowering, but further breeding resulted in varieties that did repeat flower, including 'Glastonbury', 'Othello', 'The Knight', 'The Squire', 'Wenlock' and 'Wise Portia'.

All these early roses had the true Old Rose beauty and a good fragrance. They were, however, on the whole rather weak in growth and not very healthy, in spite of the fact that their original parents were so strong. I therefore looked around for parents that were both vigorous and healthy and might at the same time be expected to retain the essential Old Rose character. My desire was to produce truly shrubby roses of natural growth although these did not necessarily have to be large in size.

First, we continued to cross our existing English Roses with further Old Roses, but these were usually drawn from the Portland Roses, the Bourbon Roses and the Hybrid Perpetual Roses. These, on the whole, were not quite so beautiful as the original Old Roses — the Gallicas and Damasks — but they did have the advantage that they were, at least in some degree, repeat flowering and like the earlier roses, had a shrubby habit of growth.

As time went by, we moved further afield for our parents, largely with health and vigour in mind. We used a number of roses that had in their ancestry *Rosa rugosa*, which is one of the three wild species that have natural repeat flowering and are also very disease resistant and vigorous. In addition, they have a strong Old Rose fragrance. All these qualities they are able to pass on to their progeny. Not only this, but in spite of the fact that *Rosa rugosa* is somewhat coarse in character, when crossed with existing English Roses, it produces varieties that are of true Old Rose character. The resulting roses are more in the spirit we desired.

There was one further quality I desired in my roses and that was diversity. If we look at the Modern Hybrid Teas, we cannot escape the fact that they are all very much of a kind. The blooms may vary in size and colour, but otherwise they differ only in small details. Since these roses are so widely grown, this seemed unfortunate. The rose is so popular and to see the same type of flower, however beautiful it may be, in every garden can become boring. This, I think, is the problem with Modern Roses; indeed, it is this that had enabled Graham Thomas to make the Old Roses popular once again. To achieve diversity, I decided to bring into my breeding roses of widely differing nature. It is well known that *Rosa wichurana* is a highly disease-resistant rose of great vigour. It gave us many of the best of our Rambler Roses and from these, shorter, repeat-flowering roses which became known as Modern Climbers. From these climbers I chose the variety 'Aloha', which, in fact, is barely a climber at all and more of a large shrub. It does, however, have cupped, rather Old Rose flowers and an excellent fragrance, together with glossy, disease-resistant foliage.

I crossed 'Aloha' with a number of existing English Roses and produced varieties a little closer to the Modern Rose with large, rather polished, dark green foliage, although the flowers were still of Old Rose shape and character. In addition, the seedlings from 'Aloha' came in a variety of colours, including yellow shades — something I very much wished to have. As a result of these crosses, we produced much larger shrubs, with large flowers to match. These included the giant-flowered 'Golden Celebration' and such large shrubs as 'Teasing Georgia'. While these roses had flowers of Old Rose formation and were very fragrant, they were something very different from our original Old Rose Hybrids. They make a very dramatic effect in the garden.

Further extending our search for diversity, we turned our attention to roses of Musk Rose origin or, at least, those that had Musk Rose in their make-up. For this purpose we used the Old Noisette Roses which were good repeaters and had flowers of delicate beauty, often with perfectly formed, rosette-shaped flowers. Their colours included white, soft pink, apricot and peach. Other roses with the Musk Roses in their parentage have also been used. One result is that these roses are nearly always fragrant, although not always with the Musk Rose scent. The reason is that this scent is found in the stamens of the flower rather than the petals and, because these roses are nearly always fully double, there are few stamens and, thus, very little of the Musk fragrance. The foliage and growth of these hybrids is quite distinct from other English Roses. They are usually more upright though not always; the leaves, too, are usually distinctive, being rather smaller than the others with pointed, light green leaflets.

Finally, we have used the Alba Roses. The Albas are a group of roses of great antiquity. They were originally the result of chance crosses between *Rosa canina* (the Dog Rose of our hedgerows) and the Gallica Roses. As might be expected, these roses are very hardy and robust. Crosses made with these roses have brought a whole new dimension to the English Roses. They are, as might be expected, much closer to the wild than our other hybrids. The flowers tend to be rather informal, yet this gives them their own special beauty. Their growth is more natural and tends towards the wild side.

This, then, is a very short survey of the development of the English Roses to date. It is, of necessity, no more than a sketch; many other crosses having been made with other classes of roses with varying degrees of success. Experimentation, needless to say, continues. Recently, we have used a whole variety of species in our search for disease-resistant roses that would not need to be sprayed with chemicals. The resulting hybrids have shown hope in this direction but, rather surprisingly, they have also yielded some very beautiful roses with pleasing growth and flowers, often quite different in character from our existing varieties. But, of course, all this takes time and developments we are making now may not be seen by the public for a few years yet.

THE CLASSIFICATION OF ENGLISH ROSES

The English Roses differ from other roses in the following respects. They are shrub roses rather than the upright bushes we have become accustomed to in the Hybrid Teas and Floribundas which were originally developed to grow in rose beds rather than the garden generally. This does not mean that English Roses are necessarily shrubs of large growth. They may sometimes be shorter than the Hybrid Teas and Floribundas, but the difference is that they have full, bushy growth, or arching growth similar to that which we might find in any other garden shrub. However, most of them are rather larger than this— around 1.2m / 4ft in height. Others may be still larger—even very large shrubs. So, as you can see, we get a great variety of growth, our idea being that roses should be of natural appearance and able to mix with other plants in the border to good effect. The flowers, too, are of all the different shapes that we find in the Old Roses and many gradations between. Their fragrance is particularly strong and beautiful and varies widely between one variety and another. The number of different fragrances we find in English Roses is far greater than in any other group of whatever age.

As a result of all this diversity, it has become obvious that English Roses need some kind of classification if gardeners are to understand them and be able to choose which variety best suits the situation in which they intend to plant them. Consequently, I have divided them into the following four groups. None of these groups has any particular botanical significance; rather, they are each of them more a collection of roses of like type. This usually means that their foundation parents were also of similar type. I should first, however, warn my reader that these groups are by no means clear-cut, one group inevitably running into the others in some degree. They are as follows: Old Rose Hybrids, The Leander Group, The English Musk Roses and The Alba Rose Hybrids.

Here I describe the English Roses that I still consider worth growing in gardens today, bearing in mind that we first introduced them half a century ago and, inevitably, many of the earlier introductions have been superseded by superior varieties. These roses were all bred by me at our Nurseries at Albrighton in Shropshire, but I have tried to be as fair in my judgement as possible. On the one hand, I may be a little biased in their favour since they are, so to speak, my 'children', and on the other hand, I probably know them better than anyone else and, as the breeder, I am or should be their severest critic.

Facing page, With its charming cupped rosette flowers of the purest deep yellow, the popular **Graham Thomas** *(foreground) forms part of the English Musk Roses group.*

English Old Rose Hybrids

These were the original English Roses. They have much of the character of the true Old Roses—the Gallicas, Damasks and so on—although they do vary widely between one variety and another. Like the Old Roses, the flowers are not flamboyant but have an unassuming charm; their colours are, in the main, beautiful soft shades of pink, crimson and purple. They usually form small bushy shrubs and repeat flower regularly. They have a strong fragrance, often of the Old Rose type. They are excellent garden roses that mingle well with other plants.

Barbara Austin is a very beautiful and very tough rose with a particularly good fragrance— a mixture of Old Rose and lilac

Barbara Austin (*Austop*) If you know the excellent 'Gertrude Jekyll', to which this rose is closely related, you will have a fair idea of this variety. It has the same, rather upright growth and Damask Rose foliage. The form of its flowers is similar, but the colour is a very soft pink and the petals have a delicate gossamer texture. It has a particularly good fragrance which can be described as a mixture of Old Rose and lilac. It has one weakness—if weakness it be— and this is that it has a tendency to send up occasional flowerless branches from the base, rather like an Old Rose, in autumn. Such branches will, of course, have flowering shoots in the following year and the shrub will be all the better for it. A very beautiful and very tough rose.

Named after my sister, Barbara Stockitt, formerly Barbara Austin, who is an authority on hardy plants. 1.1m / 3½ft. 1997.

Brother Cadfael
bears some of the largest blooms to be found among the English Old Rose hybrids

Brother Cadfael (*Ausglobe*) This rose bears some of the largest pink blooms to be found among our Old Rose Hybrids. They are deeply cupped with slightly incurved petals, providing an imposing flower which, in spite of its size, is never clumsy. Later in the season, when the plant has to carry more flowers, they may be a little smaller but are no less beautiful. The colour is a soft rose pink. There is a rich Old Rose fragrance. The growth is strong, forming a fine, medium-sized shrub. One or two blooms in a bowl of mixed roses or with other flowers will make a strong statement. Named after the detective monk in Ellis Peters' novels. 120 × 90cm / 4 × 3ft. 1990.

Charles Rennie Mackintosh (*Ausren*) Many people dislike the purple and lilac shades in roses, and I would agree with them where some Modern Roses are concerned. They are often altogether too harsh and metallic. I do not feel the same about this rose. It is of a pleasing shade of lilac—a little to the lilac side of lilac-pink. The flower formation is cupped at first, opening to form a nice rosette of medium size. They have a somewhat frilly, feminine appearance that has a definite appeal. They have a light Old Rose fragrance with aspects of almond blossom and lilac. The growth is upright, tough and wiry, with plentiful thorns and dusky foliage. It mixes well with other colours, both in the house and in the garden. Named after the designer, architect and painter. 110 × 90cm / $3\frac{1}{2}$ × 3ft. 1988.

Charles Rennie
Mackintosh has
cupped flowers that open to form frilly rosettes

Chianti (*Auswine*) A tall, broad, well formed shrub that is the result of a cross between a Gallica Rose and a Floribunda Rose. Its flowers are quite large and of fully double rosette shape; their colour a dark crimson, becoming purplish-maroon with age. There is a deep, rich Old Rose fragrance. It will be remembered that this was our first red rose which was early-summer flowering only. In spite of this, it is well worth its place in the garden. It illustrates well how, if you are willing to forgo repeat flowering in a rose, it is often possible to have a superb large shrub. This is certainly true of this rose. It will grow into a fine, very large shrub of perfect formation. Although this rose has, to some extent, been overshadowed by the better known 'Constance Spry', many people think it is rather better as a garden shrub. It was the basis from which most of the red English Roses were developed. It is, itself, quite as good as any Gallica Rose. Named after the Italian wine. Bred by David Austin and introduced jointly by Sunningdale Nurseries and David Austin Roses. 1.8 × 1.5m / 6 × 5ft. 1967.

Chianti, our first red rose, is early-summer flowering only, but well worth its place in the garden

19

Constance Spry (*Ausfirst*) This beautiful rose is to be found in the ancestry of the majority of the English Roses. It has truly magnificent flowers; in fact, they are larger than any Old Rose that I know and yet are never coarse or clumsy and are always in proportion to the shrub. Their colour is a lovely rich pink and they are of full, deep Old Rose formation, the outer petals gradually reflexing. The growth is very strong and it will, if left to its own devices, form a giant, sprawling shrub with large leaves and many thorns. It will require a good deal of space for development, growing to 2m/7ft. in height, with an equal spread and, under good conditions, even more. It is, in fact, somewhat ungainly, and is perhaps better when grown as a climber, where it will easily achieve 4.5m/15ft or more. However it is grown, it will be a magnificent sight covered with giant blooms.

The flowers have a strong fragrance, which was described by the late Graham Thomas as being similar to that of myrrh. Fragrance is hard to classify, but Graham did go to the trouble of obtaining myrrh in order to make the comparison, and he assured me his description was correct. Before the introduction of the English Roses, myrrh was a rare perfume among roses and its origin is interesting. In Graham Thomas's opinion, the myrrh fragrance originated in the Ayrshire 'Splendens' and it would appear 'Belle Isis' must have had this rose somewhere in its ancestry. It may appear to be an odd combination but, from my experience in crossing very diverse roses, I would say it is entirely possible. Be all this as it may, the particular fragrance has persisted to a remarkable degree through the generations of 'Constance Spry's' progeny. Named after Constance Spry (1886–1960) a leading pioneer of the flower arranging movement. Introduced before David Austin Roses Ltd was formed by Sunningdale Nurseries and Roses & Shrubs Limited of Albrighton. 1961.

Constance Spry was the very first of the English Roses, although not quite typical in that it does not repeat flower

Corvedale (*Ausnetting*) This is a medium-sized rose of open, cupped shape with four rings of petals. It has clear rose-pink colouring, with long, golden-yellow stamens which add greatly to its beauty. It has a strong and pleasing myrrh fragrance. The blooms are held on a rather lax shrub, which seems to suit them ideally. The whole effect is rather like that of a wild rose. A good, trouble-free garden shrub, it might be used either in a formal or less formal situation. Corvedale is a most beautiful valley running parallel to Wenlock Edge in the depths of the Shropshire countryside. 1.5 × 1.2m / 5 × 4ft. 2001.

Cottage Rose (*Ausglisten*) This rose might be said to be of the same strain as 'Mary Rose'. Its flowers are similar but perhaps of a more perfect form and a pretty rose pink with just a suggestion of an eye at the centre. It has a delicate Old Rose fragrance with hints of almond and lilac—a scent that is surprisingly diffusive when cut and placed in a warm room, or when grown in a warm climate. Its growth is upright, yet rather twiggy and bushy. Its disease resistance does not quite reach the level we would expect these days, but is easily manageable. 1.1m / 3½ft. 1991.

Facing page, **Corvedale** *is a good, trouble-free garden shrub with open, cup-shaped flowers that display long stamens*

Above, **Cottage Rose** *is one of the earlier English Roses, it has beautifully formed flowers of absolutely pure pink*

Darcey Bussell (*Ausdecorum*) Good red roses are never easy to breed, so we are particularly pleased with 'Darcey Bussell' as we believe it is one of the best and most healthy red roses we have bred to date. The flowers are not excessively large, but are produced freely and with excellent continuity. When young their outer petals form a perfect ring which later develop into a beautiful rosette. The colour is a deep rich crimson that takes on a tinge of mauve just before the petals drop. It has a

pleasing, fruity fragrance with just a hint of green. This rose, with its short bushy growth, would be an excellent shrub for the front of the border or for planting in formal rose beds and is excellent for a large pot. Darcey Bussell is the highly acclaimed ballerina. She was appointed principal at the Royal Ballet at the age of 20 and has danced in the title role of many ballets around the world. She has been honoured with many awards including the CBE in 2006. 90 x 60cm/3 x 2ft.

Darcey Bussell
bears blooms of neat rosette formation and is particularly free flowering

Eglantyne has flowers of perfect formation, with a button eye at the centre

Eglantyne (*Ausmak*) I regard this rose as one of the most beautiful of the English Old Rose Hybrids. The flowers are a lovely soft pink and of the most perfect formation, with a button eye at the centre. It is a close relation to 'Mary Rose' which it resembles, although it is a little stronger in growth and probably has a little more refinement. With all this, it has a lovely Old Rose fragrance. It is of rather upright growth without being stiff and is of medium vigour. Altogether, a most charming rose. Named after Eglantyne Jebb from Ellesmere in Shropshire, who founded the Save the Children Fund. 90cm / 3ft. 1994.

*A particularly tough variety, **England's Rose** has strongly fragrant blooms and is very weather resistant*

England's Rose (*Auslounge*) A particularly tough and reliable variety of medium size with flowers of deep glowing pink. These are shallowly cupped at first; the outer petals eventually reflexing back and revealing an attractive button eye. 'England's Rose' flowers more or less continually from June right through to the end of the season, in October or even November. The blooms are nicely held in large clusters. This is a healthy, weather-resistant rose; even in periods of continual rain the blooms do not ball and the petals drop cleanly. It will form an attractive, bushy shrub of about 120cm/4ft in height and 90cm/3ft across, although it could easily grow taller if pruned lightly. An ideal variety for planting in a rose border or for mixing with perennials. The fragrance is particularly fine; strong, warm and spicy with a classic Old Rose character. 2010.

Falstaff bears large and very impressive blooms and has a strong Old Rose fragrance to match.

Falstaff (*Ausverse*) For sheer size and colour of flower this is one of the most impressive varieties we have bred. The flowers are in the form of a cupped rosette, with numerous twisted petals within. The colour is a deep rich crimson at first, paling a little towards the outer petals—eventually becoming more of a magenta-crimson. There is an excellent, fruity, Old Rose fragrance. The foliage is quite large and tends more towards the Modern Rose than the Old. Altogether, a good and reliable, crimson rose. Named after the character in Shakespeare's *Henry IV*. Rather surprisingly, this rose does well as a climber when planted against a wall. 1.1 x 1.1m / 3½ × 3½ft. 1999.

Gentle Hermione (*Ausrumba*) I think that the outstanding feature of this rose is the perfection of its flowers. Starting as neatly rounded cups filled with petals, they develop into a perfect rosette shape. Their colour is a delicate shade of blush pink, the whole flower having an air of refinement. The growth, however, is strong—rather upright at first, gradually fanning out into a broader shrub. It has a strong Old Rose fragrance with just a hint of myrrh. It has typical Old Rose foliage which, like all our more recent roses, is highly disease-resistant. The name is taken from Shakespeare's *The Winter's Tale*. 120 × 90cm / 4 × 3ft. 2005.

Gentle Hermione
bears some of the most
perfect blooms and they are
strongly fragrant too

***Gertrude Jekyll** is a great favourite, with large flowers and one of the strongest fragrances of any rose*

Gertrude Jekyll (*Ausbord*) One of the most popular roses in our collection. The flowers are a lovely warm pink. Starting as pretty little Hybrid Tea-like buds, they develop—almost surprisingly—into well-filled rosettes with the petals spiralling from the centre, often with perfect precision. They are quite large, with the occasional giant bloom on the end of a very strong stem. They have a powerful Old Rose fragrance, such as we would expect from a Damask Rose. In fact, I can think of no other rose with quite so strong a fragrance. Growth tends to be rather upright and not particularly graceful. Gertrude Jekyll, as most of my readers will know, was one of the great influences in English gardening, and was the author of *Roses for English Gardens*.

This rose forms a shrub of medium height, but it will climb to about 2.5m / 8ft if planted against a wall. 1.5 × 1.2m / 5 × 4ft. Old Rose Hybrid. 1986.

Glamis Castle (*Auslevel*) This has almost pure white flowers, which is rather rare among garden roses. They are of cupped shape and typical Old Rose character. The growth is short and bushy with numerous twiggy branches on which it bears flowers with exceptional freedom and continuity—making it ideal for both border and bedding. There is a good English Rose myrrh fragrance. Unfortunately, it does not have quite the disease-resistance we would expect in an English Rose today, but good white roses are scarce and not easy to breed. Certainly, in drier climates or with an occasional spraying, it will perform very well and it is a beautiful rose. Named after the childhood home of the late Queen Elizabeth the Queen Mother and the setting of Shakespeare's *Macbeth*. 90cm / 3ft. 1992.

Harlow Carr (*Aushouse*) A tough little rose that bears medium-sized flowers of the most perfect formation—shallow cups of the purest rose pink. These hold their form to the end, the occasional petal falling back to give a pleasing effect. There is a strong, pure Old Rose fragrance that has been described as reminiscent of rose-based cosmetics. The plant has an excellent bushy habit, maturing into an attractively rounded shrub with its flowers extending almost to the ground—a characteristic that we particularly favour. The young foliage is bronze at first, later becoming green, the whole plant being of truly 'Old Rose' character. It is very disease-resistant. Harlow Carr, in Yorkshire, where a number of English Roses have been planted, is the most northerly of the Royal Horticultural Society gardens. 120 × 90cm / 4 × 3ft. 2004.

*Facing page, **Glamis Castle** is a particularly free flowering variety that excels in warmer, drier climates*

*Above, **Harlow Carr** has an excellent bushy habit, maturing into an attractively rounded shrub with flowers extending almost to the ground*

Heather Austin
bears cupped, chalice-shaped flowers with something of the character of an old Bourbon Rose

Heather Austin (*Auscook*) The flowers of this rose have something of the character of an old Bourbon Rose. They are a strong pink colour and distinctly cupped in shape with incurving petals. If we look inside the cup, we see golden stamens. To complete the picture, there is a strong and delicious Old Rose fragrance. Its growth is of medium height, with the flowers held well above the foliage, which tends towards the Old Rose type. It was named for my sister, now Heather Coulter. 1.2m / 4ft. 1996.

Hyde Hall (*Ausbosky*) This variety is notable for its ability to flower with exceptional continuity throughout the summer. I know of no other Shrub Rose of this size that can do this to such a degree—it really is quite exceptional in this respect. If lightly pruned, it makes a large shrub, but it can also be pruned to form a smaller shrub. It is tough and disease-resistant. The flowers are of rosette shape and medium size. Though not very showy individually, the flowers do have their own beauty and are produced with quite exceptional freedom. They are of soft pink colouring. Their delightfully warm and fruity fragrance is relatively light. The foliage is not dissimilar to that of a Dog Rose.

'Hyde Hall' is excellent for the back of a border and as a specimen in a lawn. Being particularly tough, reliable and healthy, it also makes a most attractive boundary hedge. Named after Hyde Hall, the Royal Horticultural Society garden in Essex, which includes many English Roses. 1.8 × 1.5m / 6 × 5ft. 2004.

***Hyde Hall** forms a very large shrub and flowers with exceptional continuity throughout the summer*

39

*Above, of all the English Roses **John Clare** is one of the very best for its crop of late summer/early autumn flowers*

*Facing page, **Jude the Obscure** is one of only two yellow varieties in this group and has a particularly strong and delicious fragrance reminiscent of guavas and sweet white wine*

John Clare (*Auscent*) A quite exceptional variety for its freedom of flowering especially in the summer and early autumn. The flowers are shallowly cupped and deep pink. The growth is of the type we so much favour—low, arching and broadly spreading. A good all-round rose with one drawback—it has no more than a light fragrance. Named after the rural poet who started life as a farm worker and became the finest nature poet in the English language. 80cm / 2½ft. 1994.

Jude the Obscure (*Ausjo*) I include this rose with the English Old Rose Hybrids, even though it is of rather different origin. Its flowers are yellow and, of course, we have no yellows in this group other than 'Windrush', which is one of its parents. It bears quite large, deeply cupped flowers with incurved petals, remaining this shape to the end. The colour can be described as rich yellow on the inside of the flower and pale yellow on the outside. There is a strong and unusual fragrance with a fruity note reminiscent of guava and sweet white wine, which delights all who savour her. The growth is strong and upright although bushy, with medium green leaves. Named after the character in Thomas Hardy's novel. 1.1m / 3½ft. 1995.

Kathryn Morley has some of the most beautiful blooms, perfect rosettes of pure pale pink

Kathryn Morley (*Ausclub*) This rose can no longer be included among the best of the English Roses, at least from a practical point of view. It does not quite meet our standards as regards resistance to disease—however, it is a most beautiful variety of soft rose-pink colouring and true Old Rose character. The shape is deeply cupped with petals of a delicate, almost gossamer appearance, which I think gives the flower its particular charm. Rather surprisingly, it has a Tea Rose fragrance that I would not expect in such a rose. Named after Mr and Mrs Eric Morley's daughter. $1.4 \times 1.1m / 4\frac{1}{2} \times 3\frac{1}{2}ft$. 1990.

Lady of Megginch (*Ausvolume*) With its large, richly coloured flowers, this is a particularly impressive variety. The blooms commence as pretty, rounded buds —gradually opening to form very large, full, cupped, rosette shaped flowers with the outer petals recurving back slightly. The colour is a very rich, deep pink; slightly tinged with deep orange at first and then changing to a deep rose pink. There is a good, fruity Old Rose fragrance with a definite hint of raspberry. Depending on how hard it is pruned, it will grow into a medium or large shrub of rather upright, but bushy habit. It is vigorous and healthy. A useful rose to create some excitement in a border of softer colours. Megginch Castle in Perth, Scotland is the family home of the late Baroness Strange who was President of the War Widows' Association until her death in 2005. 120 x 90cm/4 x 3ft. 2006.

Lady of Megginch is particularly impressive, with large, richly coloured flowers

L.D. Braithwaite (*Auscrim*) The English Old Rose Hybrids are notable for their lovely dusky crimsons. 'L. D. Braithwaite' is of a brighter shade which is slow to fade and, as such, it has long been a valuable rose for our collection. The flowers, which are moderately full-petalled, open wide and slightly

cupped. Their scent is not strong at first but as the flowers mature, they develop a charming Old Rose fragrance. It forms a low, rather spreading shrub that is seldom out of flower. Named after my late father-in-law. 120 × 90cm/4 × 3ft. 1988.

L.D. Braithwaite
bears some of the brightest crimson flowers in the English Roses and is seldom out of flower

Mary Magdalene is one of the very best varieties for the perfection and charm of its flowers

Mary Magdalene (*Ausjolly*) This is one of my favourite English Roses. It does not have quite the health and vigour I would like, but its flowers have a charm and beauty that it is hard to equal. They are of a soft apricot pink colour, with delicate silken petals beautifully arranged around a button eye. These petals are small at the centre, gradually becoming larger towards the outer edges. It has spreading growth with matt green, Old Rose leaves. It requires good conditions and an occasional spray to keep it growing well. It has a very beautiful Tea Rose fragrance with, rather aptly, just a hint of myrrh. Named for our local church, St Mary Magdalene, Albrighton. 90 × 90cm / 3 × 3ft. 1998.

Mary Rose (*Ausmary*) This rose was introduced at the Chelsea Flower Show in 1983 and, together with 'Graham Thomas', received a lot of attention from the media, which did much to make the English Roses known to a wider public. It is not at first sight a rose of startling beauty, but it has a modest Old Rose charm. The flowers are of medium size, informally cupped, and loosely filled with petals, their colour a strong rose pink that may be paler in the autumn. Delicious Old Rose fragrance with hints of honey and almond blossom. 'Mary Rose' forms an excellent little shrub with a bushy, branching habit of growth. The foliage is similar to that of an Old Rose. It is quite thorny. When mass planted, the pink of the flowers blends most effectively with the green of its leaves. It is very tough and can be pruned hard or allowed to grow into a larger shrub. It has produced two good sports — 'Redouté' which is a softer pink and 'Winchester Cathedral' which is white. Named on behalf of The Mary Rose Trust to mark the recovery of Henry VIII's famous flagship from the Solent after more than four hundred years. 1.2 × 1.2m / 4 × 4ft. 1983.

***Mary Rose** in a mass planting showing how the pink of the flowers blends most effectively with the green of its leaves*

*Above, **Miss Alice** is excellent for bedding or for a position towards the front of a mixed border*

*Facing page, **Mistress Quickly**, a particularly tough variety that would fit very well into the back of a mixed-border or in a semi wild area*

Miss Alice (*Ausjake*) A charming rose of true Old Rose character. The growth is quite short, but bushy. The flowers are some 8cm / 3½in across and a lovely soft pink at first, the outer petals turning to a pale pink which gradually spreads over the whole flower as it ages. An excellent rose for bedding or for a position towards the front of a mixed border. It has a lovely, well rounded Old Rose fragrance, with additional hints of Lily of the Valley. Named after Alice de Rothschild, who created a beautiful garden at Waddesdon Manor, Buckinghamshire. 90 × 60cm / 3 × 2ft. 2000.

Mistress Quickly (*Ausky*) This variety has something of the character of a Multiflora. It is a tall shrub, bearing small flowers in open sprays. These are semi-double, almost double, and medium pink with the occasional tinge of lilac. They are held well above the foliage, swaying in the wind. The foliage is matt green with small leaflets. This is a very tough variety, which could be grown in groups of three plants under semi-wild conditions to give a pleasing, natural effect. It is, insofar as I know, entirely free of disease. Named after the good-hearted character in Shakespeare's *Henry V.* 1.2m / 4ft. 1995.

*Above, **Mrs Doreen Pike** is Rugosa in appearance although the flowers are of very beautiful Old Rose form*

*Facing page, **Munstead Wood** bears flowers that become deep velvety crimson as the centre is revealed*

Mrs Doreen Pike (*Ausdor*) I am never quite sure whether I should place this rose with the Rugosas or with the English Roses. It certainly has some Rugosa in its make-up but it is, in fact, some distance removed from that group. One thing that it does have is the hardiness and disease-resistance of a Rugosa. The flowers are quite small, of rosette shape, medium pink in colour and produced on arching stems. They have a strong Old Rose fragrance. It forms a beautifully shaped, mounded shrub and is pleasing even in spring, when it produces its first leaves. Its great merit is its tough reliability and it can be depended upon to grow even in poor conditions. Doreen Pike was, for a long time, our Office Manageress at David Austin Roses and was a great stalwart in the early years. 120 × 90cm / 4 × 3ft. 1993.

Munstead Wood (*Ausbernard*) New deep crimson roses are always a welcome addition to our collection. The flowers of this variety are in fact light crimson in the bud but, as the centre gradually reveals itself, it becomes a very deep velvety crimson while the outer petals remain rather lighter in colour. They are large and cupped at first, becoming shallowly cupped with time. As the flower ages glimpses of the stigma and stamens appear amongst the petals. The growth is quite bushy, forming a broad shrub with good disease-resistance. The leaves are mid-green; the younger leaves being red-bronze to form a nice contrast. There is a strong Old Rose fragrance with a fruity note. Our fragrance expert, Robert Calkin, assesses this as 'warm and fruity with blackberry, blueberry and damson'. Munstead Wood was Gertrude Jekyll's own garden in Surrey where she worked on her many gardening books. 90 x 75cm/3 x 2.5ft. 2007.

Noble Antony (*Ausway*) This is a short, bushy rose that can be used for either bedding or at the front of a border. The colour is, I think, best described as a pleasing shade of magenta-crimson. The small incurved buds eventually develop into nicely formed, dome-shaped flowers. They have a lovely rich Old Rose scent, for which this variety was awarded the prize for fragrance at the Glasgow Trials. It has excellent lasting qualities and is ideal for arrangement in the house. Named after Mark Antony in Shakespeare's *Julius Caesar.* 90cm × 75/3 × 2½ft. 1995.

Othello (*Auslo*) Very large, deeply cupped, many-petalled dark crimson blooms that turn to shades of purple and mauve. Robust and thorny but somewhat coarse and, therefore, superseded. 1.2m/4ft. 1986.

*Facing page, **Noble Antony** is a useful rose for bedding or the front of the border, especially as it has a strong Old Rose fragrance*

*Above, **Othello** has very large, deeply cupped blooms with a deep and powerful fragrance*

Above, the flowers of
Peach Blossom *are quite large but retain great delicacy*

Facing page,
Portmeirion*, a rose of great Old Rose charm with very double flowers of pure, rich rose pink*

Peach Blossom (*Ausblossom*) Here we have a rose of supreme delicacy and refinement. Although the blooms are quite large, they are produced very freely and nicely poised on airy growth. They are of sheeny pink colouring and their massed effect does, to me at least, have a blossom-like quality. A good shrubby rose of 1.2m / 4ft in height. 1990.

Portmeirion (*Ausgard*) Perhaps the most outstanding virtue of this rose is the nature of its growth, which is in many ways ideal. It grows to about 90cm / 3ft in height and is of equal width, with very full growth, so that we get a small mound which flowers almost to the ground. The flowers are of typical Old Rose character and of rich pink colouring; they are rosette in shape with numerous small petals enclosed within two formal rings of larger outer petals. They have a rich Old Rose fragrance. Unfortunately, it has recently shown a slight tendency to blackspot and may require spraying. Named for Susan Williams-Ellis, who was well known for her beautiful Portmeirion Pottery. She always took great interest in the development of English Roses. 90 × 90cm / 3 × 3ft. 1999.

__Princess Alexandra of Kent__ a relatively new variety with very large flowers and a strong and delicious fragrance

Princess Alexandra of Kent (*Ausmerchant*) We are very honoured to name this rose for Princess Alexandra, who is a cousin to Queen Elizabeth II. She is a keen gardener and great lover of roses. The rose that bears her name has unusually large flowers of a warm, glowing pink. They are full-petalled and deeply cupped in shape, all enclosed in a ring of outer petals of a softer pink; creating a most pleasing effect. In spite of their size they are never clumsy, being held nicely poised on a well-rounded shrub of 1.0m/3.5ft in height and 75cm/2.5ft across. Because of their size, there is a lot to be said for planting in groups of three, keeping both flowers and growth nicely balanced. They have a delicious fresh Tea fragrance which interestingly changes completely to lemon as the flower ages — eventually taking on additional hints of blackcurrants. It is very healthy. 2007.

***Redouté** is a soft pink sport of 'Mary Rose', with a bushy, branching habit of growth*

Redouté (*Auspale*) A sport of 'Mary Rose' and similar in every way, except that it is a lovely soft pink. Named after Pierre Joseph Redouté (1759–1840) the most famous of all rose painters. 1.2m / 4ft. 1992.

Rosemoor (*Austough*) A particularly charming little rose that bears small, perfectly formed, rosette-shaped flowers that remind one of the old Centifolia Rose 'De Meaux'. The colour is a lovely soft pink, deeper at the centre and lighter towards the edges. As the flower ages it pales a little and reveals a tiny green eye, which provides a most pleasing effect. There is a strong fragrance that seems to suit the character of the flower perfectly. This is basically an Old

Rose fragrance, with additional hints of apple, cucumber and violet leaf. 'Rosemoor' is quite upright in growth, yet bushy and it flowers with remarkable freedom and continuity. It is also very disease-resistant. All in all, a rose of true Old Rose character in flower, leaf and growth. It is an ideal rose for the front of the border or for a more formal setting, where its beauty and fragrance can be appreciated to the full. Named after the beautiful Royal Horticultural Society garden in Devon, which has done so much to dispel the idea that roses cannot be grown in the south west of the British Isles. Rosemoor includes many English Roses that grow very well. 110×80cm / $3\frac{1}{2} \times 2\frac{1}{2}$ft. 2004.

***Rosemoor** is a very charming rose with rosette-shaped flowers and a most delicious fragrance*

St. Swithun (*Auswith*) In common with a number of other English Roses, this variety was first introduced as a shrub but is now more often grown as a climber. Nonetheless, it is still true to say that it is very valuable in both roles. The flowers, which are soft pink in colour, are beautifully formed in an almost perfect flat rosette, the shape being naturally rounded and unusually full of very small petals. They have a strong myrrh fragrance. The growth is tall yet bushy, with leaves of a greyish-green. It has a good health record. A rose of great charm. Named to commemorate the 900th anniversary of Winchester Cathedral. 1.2 x 1.0m/4 x 3½ft. or 2.5m/8ft. as a climber. 1993.

Sharifa Asma (*Ausreef*) A rose of great delicacy and beauty. The flowers are of slightly incurved rosette formation, soft pink with a touch of gold at the base of the petals, the outer petals paling with age. These are resistant to rain but can be damaged by very hot sun. The strong fragrance has fruity notes reminiscent of white grapes and mulberry. All in all, they have a gentle, translucent quality which is most appealing. The growth is upright and bushy. Sharifa Asma is a Princess of the Omani Royal Family. 110 × 80cm / 3½ × 2½ft. 1989.

*Facing page, **St. Swithun** was first introduced as a shrub but is now more often grown as a climber—valuable in both roles*

*Above, **Sharifa Asma** has petals with a translucent quality, and a strong fragrance reminiscent of white grapes and mulberry*

*Above, **Sir Walter Raleigh** has large flowers of pure rose pink borne on vigorous, slightly arching stems*

*Facing page, **Sister Elizabeth** is a little rose of low, broad growth that forms a neat mound and may also be grown as a short, neat hedge within the garden*

Sir Walter Raleigh (*Ausspry*) This is a large and generous rose with flowers rather like those of a tree peony, some 12cm / 5in across, not quite fully double, opening wide and slightly cupped, and usually showing their stamens. They are a lovely warm pink and have a strong Old Rose fragrance. The growth is tall and strong and the foliage large, with everything in proportion to the flowers although disease resistance is rather lacking. Named to mark the 400th anniversary of the founding of the first English-speaking colony in America. 1.5 × 1.2m / 5 × 4ft.1985.

Sister Elizabeth (*Auspalette*) A charming little rose of low, neatly rounded growth which arches and branches freely to form a symmetrical mound. The flowers are of similar character to an old Gallica Rose; perfectly formed rosettes, each with a button eye at the centre. Their colour is rose pink with a distinct lilac tinge. They have a sweet, spicy, Old Rose fragrance. An excellent rose for the front of the border, where it will mingle beautifully with perennials or other plants. It may also be grown as a short, neat hedge within the garden. An ideal subject for growing in pots and other containers. Sister Elizabeth is a Cistercian nun from the Holy Cross Abbey in Whitland, South Wales. She has long been a great rose lover. 75 x 75cm/2.5 x 2.5ft.

Sophy's Rose forms a shapely shrub that is ideal for the front of a border, or for growing in rose beds

Sophy's Rose (*Auslot*) The flowers start as pretty cups, opening to form attractive, light red rosettes of medium size with a soft Tea Rose fragrance. It forms a shapely little shrub of healthy, twiggy growth. An ideal plant for the front of a border, or for growing in rose beds especially as it repeat flowers so well. Disease-resistance is good for a red rose. Named on behalf of the Dyslexia Institute after the daughter of its founder, Wendy Fisher. 90 × 80cm / 3 × 2½ft. 1997.

Spirit of Freedom (*Ausbite*) The flowers of this rose start as small, rounded buds which gradually open to form a cupped flower, well filled with numerous small, spiralling petals that are slightly dished towards the centre. The colour is a lovely soft pink which gradually turns to lilac-pink as the flower ages. There is a pleasing fragrance with a hint of myrrh. A rose of charming Old Rose beauty that will form a substantial shrub. It is highly disease-resistant. We were pleased to name this rose for The Freedom Association, which does much good work campaigning for the preservation and extension of freedom. $1.5 \times 1.2m/5 \times 4ft$. While this rose forms an excellent shrub, it is perhaps even better as a climber reaching a height of about 2.5m/8ft. 2002.

Susan Williams-Ellis (*Ausquirk*) The Mayflower was introduced in 2001 and has become a firm favourite with its charming rosette shaped flowers of pure rose pink, strong fragrance and of course its extremely good health. It remained stable until 5 or 6 years ago but then suddenly a stem with pure white flowers appeared: this is the result. The remarkable thing about these two roses is that insofar as we are aware they are completely free from disease and also start to flower so early in the season—usually late May or early June at our Shropshire nursery and then continuing almost without stop until the harder frosts. For those in a really cold climate, it is also extremely winter hardy. Good white roses are particularly difficult to breed and so we are particularly delighted to have found this variety. The fragrance is strong and perfectly Old Rose in character. Ideal for the border, for hedging or for a container. A delightful, unassuming little rose of typical Old Rose beauty. Susan Williams-Ellis was a designer who, together with her husband Euan Cooper-Willis, founded Portmeirion Pottery. Susan was a great enthusiast of the English Roses and painted some beautiful watercolours of them. 120 x 90cm/4 x 3ft. 2010.

Susan Williams-Ellis is sport of The Mayflower with all the same characteristics of extreme health, free flowering and strong fragrance

*Facing page, **Spirit of Freedom** is a rose of charming Old Rose beauty that will form a sub-stantial shrub or even better a climber*

Tam o'Shanter is a big rose and so suitable for a semi wild area or at the back of a wide mixed border

Tam o'Shanter (*Auscerise*) 'Tam o'Shanter' is very different to the other English Roses and we hardly know in which group to place it. The growth is long and gracefully arching; the flowers opening all along their length, rather as we might get on a Species Rose. The individual blooms are initially of typical Old Rose formation, being rosette shaped later opening up to reveal the stamens. The colour is a deep cerise pink that takes on a slightly mauve shade when the flower is fully open. There is a light fruity fragrance. It is very healthy. This is a rose that would look very well in an informal garden or as part of a mixed border. It was named to commemorate the 250th anniversary of the birth of Robbie Burns. Tam o'Shanter is the hero of one of his best known poems, in which he has a lucky escape from the witches having stayed too long at the inn after market day. 1.8 x 1.5m/6 x 5ft. 2009.

Tess of the d'Urbervilles is very free flowering and is the brightest crimson of the English Roses

Tess of the d'Urbervilles (*Ausmove*) The large, fragrant flowers of bright crimson colouring are deeply cupped in the early stages and open to a looser, but still pleasing, shape, the petals turning back with age to look even more informal. The weight of the flowers bows down the branches, giving an elegant effect. The growth is robust, bushy and spreading and the foliage large and of a dark green. Rather surprisingly for a shrub of this size, it will form a good short climber. Named after the well-known character in Thomas Hardy's novel. 1.2 x 1.2m/4 x 4ft. or 2.5m/8ft. as a climber. 1998.

The Countryman
is a very beautiful and healthy rose with a particularly delicious Old Rose and strawberry fragrance

The Countryman (*Ausman*) Like 'Gertrude Jekyll', this is a cross between an English Rose and a Portland rose and it may be helpful to refer back to my remarks on 'Gertrude Jekyll'. The flowers are quite large, loosely double rosettes, deep pink in colour, with an exceptionally fruity Old Rose fragrance. For me, they have something of the spirit of the peonies we see in Chinese and Japanese paintings, both in character and the way in which they grow on the plant, although they are, in reality, much smaller. The leaves have something of the character of a Portland Rose, quite large with well spaced leaflets, and exceptionally healthy. It is important to remove the dead flowers to encourage quick new growth, and we can then expect two good periods of flower, although there will only be occasional blooms in between. 90 x 100cm/3 x 3½ft. 1987.

The Dark Lady loves warmer climates where it is one of the most magnificent of all red varieties

The Dark Lady (*Ausbloom*) A dark crimson rose with large, rather loosely formed, wide open flowers of rosette shape. These have a rather special character which reminds me of the flowers of a tree peony. They have a true Old Rose fragrance. They are held on a rounded, bushy shrub. Useful as a crimson rose that is particularly happy in warmer climates. In Britain it has a slight tendency to blackspot. It is particularly successful and a great favourite in the southern states of the USA and other areas with warmer, drier climates although here it becomes a deep pink in the sun. The name is taken from the 'dark lady' of Shakespeare's sonnets. 1.1m / 3½ft. 1991.

The Herbalist (*Aussemi*) This variety was named for its similarity to *Rosa gallica* var. *Officinalis*, often known as the Apothecary's Rose, the great difference being that 'The Herbalist' is repeat flowering. It has the same simple beauty. It is a semi-double rose that opens wide and flat, exposing a large bunch of golden stamens. I would describe the colour of the flower as light crimson, varying to dark pink. It is a strong and reliable rose of bushy habit and typical Old Rose character. It is an ideal border plant. There is a light fragrance. 90 × 90cm / 3 × 3ft. 1991.

The Herbalist
was named for its similarity to Rosa gallica *var.* Officinalis *although it repeat flowers very well*

The Mayflower
represents an important breakthrough in English Roses

The Mayflower (*Austilly*) This rose represents an important breakthrough in English Roses: it is, we believe, virtually free of disease. Even when it gets the odd touch of blackspot, it seems to have the ability to kill this off at an early stage. Unfortunately, in warmer parts of the world it has a tendency to suffer from red spider, although this is not a problem in Britain. You never quite win them all! It is the first of the English Roses to start flowering and continues with great regularity through to the autumn. The flowers have a typical Old Rose charm and are of medium size, rosette-shaped, with a strong Old Rose fragrance. The growth is full, bushy and rather upright, with numerous twiggy branches and quite small, matt green foliage, which is also of Old Rose appearance. This is a very useful rose in the garden, where it can be placed towards the front of the border. It is very tough and hardy. I have seen 'The Mayflower' looking very pleasing in north Shropshire. We named this rose to mark the launch of our American branch at Tyler in Texas. 120 × 90cm / 4 × 3ft. 2001.

Trevor Griffiths (*Ausold*) Like 'The Countryman' and 'Barbara Austin', this rose has a strong streak of the old Portland Rose in its breeding. All three roses have foliage and growth that leans heavily towards the Old Roses in character. They also all have a wonderful Old Rose fragrance which, in this particular variety, has been described as reminiscent of old claret. The blooms are of beautiful formation, opening as perfect, flat, well-filled rosettes that are deep pink, paling a little towards the edges. Its disease-resistance leaves a little to be desired, but no more than we would find in an Old Rose—and it can be controlled by an occasional spraying. Named after Trevor Griffiths, the well-known New Zealand rose grower, who has done so much to introduce Old Roses to that country and is also the author of a number of beautiful books. 110×90cm / $3\frac{1}{2} \times 3$ft. 1994.

***Trevor Griffiths**, a variety with an outstanding Old Rose fragrance, reminiscent of old claret*

*An extremely tough rose, **Wild Edric** can withstand very difficult situations but still keep on flowering*

Wild Edric (*Aushedge*) This is an unusually tough and reliable rose that will thrive even under difficult conditions and is not only suitable for the border but also useful for semi-wild planting or for hedges. It has quite a lot of *Rosa rugosa* in its breeding and this makes it not quite a typical English Rose. The flowers are large, semi-double and substantial. They are held in close clusters, each bloom opening in succession. Their colour is deep pink with a purple tinge at first, paling a little with age. They have a bunch of contrasting golden stamens. The fragrance is strong and delicious, but interestingly, with a little investigation, a marked difference between the fragrance of the petals and the stamens can be detected. The scent of the stamens is pure clove, whereas that of the petals is classic Old Rose with hints of watercress and cucumber. This is a very tough and reliable rose that will grow well even under poor conditions and, exceptionally in the rose world, is not eaten by deer. Wild Edric was a Saxon Lord in Shropshire, who was said to have married a fairy queen. He reproached her one day and she disappeared. Legend has it that his ghost is still to be seen searching for her in the hills. 1.2×1.2m / 4×4ft. 2005.

*Above, **Winchester Cathedral**, one of the few truly white flowered English Roses*

*Facing page, **William Shakespeare 2000**, has superb, strongly fragrant crimson blooms and attractive bushy growth*

William Shakespeare 2000 (*Ausromeo*) This variety bears superb blooms of a deep, rich velvety crimson that gradually turns into an equally rich purple. The flowers are cupped at first, eventually opening to a shallow cup with nicely quartered petals. They are of strongly Old Rose character and are set against typical Old Rose foliage. To complement these characteristics, they have the strong, warm Old Rose fragrance that we expect—but do not always find—in roses of this colour. The growth is strong, bushy and attractively spreading in habit. It has good disease-resistance, particularly for a red rose. There is a large bed of 'William Shakespeare' roses and a mixed border of English and other roses at Shakespeare's birthplace in Stratford-upon-Avon, Warwickshire. 110 × 80cm / 3½ × 2½ft. 2000.

Winchester Cathedral (*Auscat*) A sport of 'Mary Rose' and similar in every way, except that it has flowers of pure white; a fact that makes it most valuable since there are at present very few white-flowered varieties among the English Roses. Named in aid of The Winchester Cathedral Trust. 1.2 × 1.2m / 4 × 4ft. 1998.

*Above, **Windrush**, a vigorous and particularly free flowering shrub, if not dead headed it will bear an excellent crop of hips*

*Facing page, **Young Lycidas**, a magnificent variety with large strongly coloured flowers and a delicious fragrance to match*

Windrush (*Ausrush*) Not quite a typical English Old Rose Hybrid in character, but this variety represents a first attempt to bring yellow to these roses. The flowers are large, semi-double and of soft yellow colouring, with plentiful dark yellow stamens. There is a light, spicy Musk fragrance. The growth is strong and bushy and the foliage has something of the Old Rose character. There is a tendency to produce fine large hips which, though beautiful, tend to curb future flowering. These can be removed if you require a better crop of later flowers. Named after the river in southern England. $1.2 \times 1.2m / 4 \times 4ft$. 1984.

Young Lycidas (*Ausvibrant*) This is a variety of classic Old Rose beauty. The flowers are quite large and deeply cupped even when fully open; the many petals arranged in a charming, rather informal way. Their colour is new to English Roses; a blend of very deep magenta, pink and red — the outer petals tending towards light purple — although this is in contrast to the outside of the petals, which are quite silvery in appearance. The flowers nod gracefully and are produced singly or in small groups on vigorous stems. Its growth will build up to form an attractive, bushy shrub of perhaps 1.2m/4ft tall by 90cm/3ft across. There is a delicious fragrance that changes markedly with the age of the flower; starting as a pure Tea scent and changing to a blend of Tea and Old Rose, with intriguing hints of cedar wood. 'Young Lycidas' would be an excellent choice to associate with English Roses and Old Roses in a rose border or in a mixed border with perennials. Friends of the John Milton Society asked us to name this rose to mark the 400th anniversary of the birth of the poet John Milton. His poem *Lycidas* ends on a note of hopefulness, with the words 'Tomorrow to fresh Woods, and Pastures new'. Interestingly, it was Milton who introduced the word 'fragrance' into the English language. 2008.

The Leander Group

The Leander group of English Roses is the result of once again crossing varieties of our Old Rose Hybrids with more modern varieties, often with *Rosa wichurana* in their make-up. The result is that we have a group of English Roses that lean a little more towards the Modern Rose, while their flowers are still of typical Old Rose formation. They usually form large, robust shrubs with elegantly arching growth. The flowers are often large and gracefully poised on the branch, providing a most pleasing effect. The colours are wide-ranging, including many rich yellows, apricots and some flame shades. Their fragrance is strong and varied—sometimes of the Old Rose type, sometimes Tea Rose or myrrh. These scents are frequently mixed with fruity notes such as raspberry, lemon or apple.

A Shropshire Lad (*Ausled*) Altogether one of our best varieties, this is most often grown as a climber but it is also very good when grown as a large shrub placed well back in the border. Its flowers are soft peachy pink and slightly cupped at first; becoming rosette-shaped—the petals turning back at the edges. They have a delicious Tea Rose fragrance. The foliage is large, of typical modern Leander character and very healthy. $1.8 \times 1.5\text{m}/6 \times 5\text{ft}$. This rose is equally good when grown as a climber, when it will cover a large area and reach a height of $2.5\text{m}/8\text{ft}$ or more. We have a particularly fine example of it growing on an arch. The name comes from A. E. Housman's 'A Shropshire Lad'. 1996.

A Shropshire Lad bears rosette-shaped blooms, the petals turning back at the edges

Abraham Darby
has large, deeply cupped flowers and forms a large bush with long, arching growth

Abraham Darby (*Auscot*) This variety is unusual among English Roses in that it is the result of a cross between two roses that bear flowers similar to those of an Old Rose but are nevertheless Modern: the Floribunda 'Yellow Cushion' and 'Aloha', a Modern Climber. 'Abraham Darby' is very much a Shrub Rose, forming a large bush with long, arching growth and large, glossy leaves. The flowers, in spite of the parentage, are of truly Old Rose formation: large, deeply cupped and loosely filled with petals. The colour is soft peachy pink on the inside of the petals and a pale yellow on the outside. The centre petals fold and turn inwards to give a mixture of yellow and pink. All these colours fade towards the edge of the flower as it ages, providing a soft and pleasing effect. There is a delicious, strong and fruity fragrance with a raspberry sharpness. It is hardy, disease resistant and recurrent flowering. $1.5 \times 1.5m / 5 \times 5ft$. 1985.

__Alan Titchmarsh__ bears deeply cupped flowers that, despite their size and opulence, look completely 'right' on the bush

Alan Titchmarsh (*Ausjive*) We are always looking for better varieties with flowers of a deeply cupped shape. In 'Alan Titchmarsh' we have a prime example of such a rose. The blooms are indeed of deeply cupped form, tending to incurve a little even when fully open, with numerous small, similarly incurved petals in the centre—their colour a deep pink, slightly paler on the outer petals—and they are displayed slightly nodding on a well rounded yet nicely arching shrub. They have a strong Old Rose fragrance with a hint of myrrh. Despite their size and opulence, they look completely 'right' on the bush. It has dark green, typically Leander foliage. Named after the well-known television horticulturist, who has been an inspiration to gardeners over many years. It is also known as the Huntington Rose in North America after the wonderful Huntington Library in California and where some of the very first English Roses were planted in the States in the mid 1980s. 120 × 90cm / 4 × 3ft. 2005.

Ambridge Rose (*Auswonder*) This is a good all-round garden rose. It flowers very freely and continuously, has bushy, rather upright growth and can equally well be used for a border as for a rose bed. The flowers are of medium size, nicely cupped at first, opening to a loose rosette formation; their colour is deep apricot at the centre, paling to the outer edges of the flower. Strong and delicious fragrance. Named at the request of the BBC for their long-running *The Archers* serial. $110 \times 60\text{cm} / 3^1/_2 \times 2\text{ft}$. 1990.

Ambridge Rose *is a good all-round garden rose that flowers very freely and continuously*

89

Benjamin Britten
is a very lively colour that
is never loud and is ideal
for mixing with other
English Rose colours

Benjamin Britten (*Ausencart*) The unusual feature of this rose is its colour, which I find almost impossible to describe. The best I can say is that it is as though you had mixed scarlet paint with a little orange or perhaps as soft scarlet. However you describe it, it is, I think, a beautiful and very lively colour that is never loud and is ideal for mixing with other English Rose colours, both in the garden and in a bowl of cut roses. The flower starts as a cup, soon opening to form a cupped rosette. The fragrance is intensely fruity, with aspects of wine and pear drops. The growth is strong and rather upright, bearing its flowers mainly at the top. Named to commemorate the life and work of the famous English composer, conductor and performer. 120×90cm / 4×3ft. 2001.

Charles Austin (*Ausfather*) A strong, upright shrub with large, shiny modern foliage and bearing exceptionally large, full-petalled flowers of an apricot-yellow colouring paling with age and becoming very slightly tinged with pink. Strong, fruity fragrance. Although it does not repeat continuously, it can be relied on to provide a second crop in the autumn. It is perhaps a little coarse when put alongside our more recent productions, but can be impressive towards the back of a border, where it will grow much taller if lightly pruned. For other positions it is better cut down to half its height if it is not to become ungainly. Named after my father. Height 1.2–1.8m / 4–6ft. 1973. 'Yellow Charles Austin' is a sport of this variety which is similar in every way except for colour.

Charles Austin, a very tough rose, it is extremely popular in Germany and Scandinavian countries

Charles Darwin
bears flowers that face upwards and are some of the largest among English Roses

Charles Darwin (*Auspeet*) The flowers of this variety are some of the largest among English Roses. While we would not want all roses to be of such a size, it is good to have some to use where a really bold effect is required. The blooms are full and deeply cupped at first, but open to a rather shallower flower, usually revealing a button eye. There is a strong and delicious fragrance which varies, according to weather conditions, between a soft floral Tea Rose and almost pure lemon. The colour could be described as yellow, tending towards

mustard. All in all, this is an impressive and eye-catching shrub with broad, spreading growth, the flowers facing upwards on the ends of long stems. Vigorous and disease-resistant. Named after the scientist whose revolutionary work on evolution changed the course of history. He was born in Shrewsbury, Shropshire, not far from our nursery. $1.2 \times 1.1\text{m}/4 \times 3\frac{1}{2}\text{ft}$. 2003.

Christopher Marlowe (*Ausjump*) A new shade among English Roses— intense orange-red, paling a little as the flower ages—that is not usually associated with English Roses, but we need all colours to fulfil the various requirements of the garden colour scheme. 'Christopher Marlowe' is useful where a bright splash of red is required. The flowers are rosette-shaped; the outer petals reflexing a little and paling slightly with age. They have a pleasing Tea Rose fragrance with a hint of lemon. The growth is short but very vigorous, with numerous stems arising from the base and later branching to give a continuous flow of flowers. The overall effect is that of a nicely rounded shrub. It is a very healthy rose. Christopher Marlowe, the well-known playwright and contemporary of William Shakespeare, is said to have pressed a rosebud in a book as a mark of friendship to someone with whom he had had an argument. $90 \times 90\text{cm}/3 \times 3\text{ft}$. 2002.

Christopher Marlowe makes a bright splash of orange-red, the blooms borne with excellent continuity

93

Above, **Crown Princess Margareta** *has tall, vigorous, slightly arching growth and thrives even under difficult conditions*

Facing page, **Cymbeline** *has the pure myrrh fragrance, found almost only in the English Roses*

Crown Princess Margareta (*Auswinter*) The colour of this variety may be described as bright apricot-orange, which is a lovely shade that shows up across the garden, and this rose is certainly one of the finest in this range of colours. The flowers are quite large and of rosette shape. The plant is tall, vigorous and slightly arching—typical of the group—with ample dark green foliage. It will thrive even under more difficult conditions. There is a strong, fruity fragrance of the Tea Rose type. Crown Princess Margareta of Sweden was a granddaughter of Queen Victoria and an accomplished landscape gardener. This variety is even more beautiful when grown as a climber on a wall, fence, arch or obelisk where it will reach a height of 2.5m/8ft. 1999.

Cymbeline Large flowers of 10cm/4in or more across, opening flat and loosely filled with petals. The colouring is most unusual, a greyish almost ashen pink with tinges of brown. Although this may not please everyone, I find it beautiful and think it could be useful in garden colour schemes. The growth arches to the ground in an elegant manner showing the flowers to maximum effect. It is truly recurrent flowering and has a strong myrrh fragrance. Height 1.2m/4ft. 1982.

Geoff Hamilton (*Ausham*) This variety has lovely soft pink flowers that pale towards the outer petals. Starting as a very full, cupped shape, they gradually evolve into a full-petalled rosette formation. They have an Old Rose scent with just a hint of apple. 'Geoff Hamilton' will grow into a large shrub suitable for

the back of a border. The foliage is typically 'Leander', glossy and disease-resistant. A beautiful and very practical rose that combines delicacy and refinement with exceptional vigour and health. Named after the well-known and much-loved television gardener. 120 x 90cm/4 x 3ft. 1997.

Geoff Hamilton
forms a vigorous and healthy shrub bearing plentiful blooms and with glossy and disease-resistant foliage, seen here with false mallow (Sidalcea)

Facing page, **Golden Celebration** *is an excellent all-round variety, ideal with other shrubs in a border*

Above, **Grace** *has numerous unusually narrow petals that give the flower a very different appearance*

Golden Celebration (*Ausgold*) I have always taken the view that sheer size of bloom is no great virtue in a rose, yet this is one of the largest-flowered of the English Roses. They are in the form of magnificent golden cups which hold their shape to the end. In spite of their size, they are never ungainly. I think this is because they are so gracefully held, slightly nodding, on long, arching branches. They have a strong Tea scent at first, later developing hints of Sauternes wine and strawberry. The shrub itself is quite big and is of a suitable size for the flower. Later in the season, we can expect a larger crop of flowers but these will be rather smaller and not quite so deeply cupped. The foliage is large, glossy, light green and resistant to disease. $1.2 \times 1.2m / 4 \times 4ft$. 1992.

Grace (*Auskeppy*) A rose with a strong individuality due, I think, to its unusually narrow petals that give the flower a very different appearance. These petals are numerous and gradually turn back to form a large, domed rosette with the hint of a button eye. Their colour is a lovely shade of apricot—deeper in the centre—and fading almost to white at the edges. All this provides us with flowers that are both charming and elegant. There is a delicious warm and sensuous fragrance. The blooms are held on an excellent shrub of rather broad, arching growth. It is vigorous, healthy and repeat flowers well. In every way, an excellent garden plant. $1.2 \times 1.2m / 4 \times 4ft$. 2001.

*Above, **James Galway**, a superb, large shrub with long, slightly arching, almost thornless growth and neat, domed flowers*

*Facing page, **Janet** has long, elegant, typical Hybrid Tea buds which open gradually to become shapely rosettes*

James Galway (*Auscrystal*) A superb, large shrub with long, slightly arching, almost thornless growth—typical of our Leander group. This is a tough, disease-free rose that is excellent for the back of a mixed border. The flowers are quite large and very full, with many petals arranged in a neat formation, the petals eventually turning back so that the rose becomes almost ball-like. The colour is a lovely warm pink at the centre, shading to pale pink at the edges. There is a delicious Old Rose fragrance. Named in celebration of the 60th birthday of James Galway, the world-famous flautist. An excellent shrub rose and equally good as a climber when it will reach a height of 2.5m/8ft and flower all the way from top to bottom. 2000.

Janet (*Auspishus*) For many years we have been breeding roses with open flowers of the Old Rose type. Some people may be a little surprised to find that in 'Janet' we return to a flower of the Hybrid Tea type. The difference is that whereas the Hybrid Teas are beautiful in the bud, they tend to lack form in the later stages. 'Janet' has long, elegant, typical Hybrid Tea buds which open gradually to become shapely rosettes, so that we get the benefit of both types of flower in one rose. The colour in the bud is a delightful mixture of pale and deep pinks flushed with copper, the underside of the petals being soft yellow. As it opens into a rosette shape, the flower becomes a deep glowing pink, paling a little towards the outside of the petals. Another equally important difference is that 'Janet' is not a short bush as we would expect with a Hybrid Tea, but a shrub with long, arching growth that holds its flowers beautifully—each bud hanging elegantly towards us on a long stem. There is a lovely, strong pure Tea Rose fragrance. Named for Janet, in her memory, who had a life-long love of roses. The family didn't want any publicity so no mention of surname. $1.2 \times 1.1m/4 \times 3\frac{1}{2}ft$. It forms a good climber of some 2.5m/8ft. 2003.

Jubilee Celebration (*Aushunter*) We were very pleased to name this rose in commemoration of the Queen's Golden Jubilee in 2002. It is a large, impressive flower, of domed shape and of a lovely rich salmon pink tinted with gold on the underside of the petals, the blooms being held well above its lush foliage. Despite the size of the flowers, they are produced with exceptional freedom and continuity. The growth is vigorous, building up into a fine large shrub. There is a deliciously fruity rose scent often strongly lemon or even lemon zest with hints of raspberry. It is very healthy. Altogether, a most impressive rose. $1.2 \times 1.2\text{m}/4 \times 4\text{ft}$. 2002.

Jubilee Celebration bears impressive, large flowers of domed shape and is healthy and reliable. Shown here with Astilbe *'Broncelaub'*

***Lady of Shalott**, an extremely free flowering and reliable variety creating a wonderful display in the garden*

Lady of Shalott (*Ausnyson*) This rose promises to be one of the most robust and hardy roses in our collection. It is also highly resistant to disease and it will bloom with unusual continuity throughout the season. Indeed, it is an ideal rose for the inexperienced gardener. The young buds are a rich orange-red. These open to form chalice-shaped blooms, filled with loosely-arranged petals. Each petal has a salmon pink upper side which contrasts beautifully with the attractive golden-yellow reverse. The chalice shape means that the undersides of the petals are clearly seen, revealing glimpses of the deeper colour in the heart of the bloom. There is a pleasant, warm, tea fragrance, with hints of spiced apple and cloves. Lady Of Shalott quickly forms a large, bushy shrub with slightly arching stems. The mid-green leaves have attractive, slightly bronzed tones when young. The Tennyson Society asked us to name this rose to commemorate the 200th anniversary of his birth in 2009. The name is taken from one of Alfred, Lord Tennyson's favourite poems. In the poem, the Lady of Shalott lived in a castle close to King Arthur's Camelot and was held in a spell until she saw the reflection of Sir Lancelot in a mirror. 1.2 x 1.0m/4 x 3.5ft. 2009.

Leander, one of the early English Roses and the variety that gave its name to this group, it is a particularly tough rose

Leander (*Auslea*) The variety that gave its name to this group of roses is no longer one of the most beautiful but it is certainly one of the toughest and most reliable, and will thrive even under difficult conditions. Its deep apricot flowers are small to medium in size, rosette-shaped and tightly packed with petals. They are held in small sprays. The foliage is shiny, disease-resitant and of modern appearance. There is a delightful raspberry scent in the Tea Rose tradition. 2.1 × 1.5m / 7 × 5ft. Named after the legendary Greek lover. It also forms a good climber. 1982.

Lilian Austin (*Ausmound*) A small garden shrub of an excellent, spreading, bushy habit and one which looks very much in place with other plants in the border. The flowers are semi-double, at times almost double, opening wide to show their stamens, while their petals are slightly waved. The colour is a strong salmon-pink, shading to yellow at the centre. 'Lilian Austin' is hardy, disease resistant and reliably repeat flowering and it has a good fragrance. Named after my mother. 120 × 90cm / 4 × 3ft. 1973.

Morning Mist (*Ausfire*) Being a large and vigorous, single-flowered shrub, this variety is ideal for a place at the back of the border where its flowers can be clearly seen well above other subjects to pleasing effect. The colour is deep pink at first, opening to a bright salmon pink with yellow at the centre. There is a large boss of golden stamens with red anthers. The fragrance is light and a mixture of musk and cloves. Later in the season it bears a wonderful crop of large red hips. The growth is very strong and healthy, with foliage of a rather modern appearance. 1.8m/6ft. 1996.

Morning Mist is ideal for a place at the back of the border where its single flowers can be clearly seen above other subjects

Pat Austin, *a brilliant shade of copper, but in no way gaudy, illustrates the seemingly endless variety of form of which the rose is capable. The catmint,* Nepeta *'Six Hills Giant', provides good contrast*

Pat Austin (*Ausmum*) If you are one of those rose lovers who prefer pinks, blushes and reds in English and Old Roses, then it is worthwhile thinking again as regards this rose. Although the colour can only be described as a brilliant shade of copper, it is in no way gaudy. Perhaps this is because the inside of the petals is copper, while the outside is a coppery-yellow. Light shining through the petals creates a soft glow that is quite entrancing. The flower is large, well-rounded and loosely petalled, providing an effect that is different from that of any other English Rose. This illustrates very well the great and seemingly endless form of which the rose is capable. The scent has been described as a strong Tea Rose fragrance with a warm, sensuous background. The shrub is tall and slightly arching, with the flowers held elegantly on the branch. The foliage is dark and of the kind we expect from a Leander rose. This beautiful rose is named after my wife. 1.2m / 4ft. 1995.

Princess Anne (*Auskitchen*) An exciting new development, stemming from an entirely new line in breeding. It has an overall character that is very different from any other rose we know, having its own very special beauty yet retaining the classic full-petalled flowers of an English Rose. The young flower is deep pink, almost red, gradually fading to a pure deep pink as the bloom matures. The undersides of the petals have a pleasing hint of yellow. The growth is upright and the foliage is quite thick, succulent and highly polished and

remarkably resistant to disease. It flowers over a long period and in large clusters; the individual blooms opening in succession. There is a Tea Rose fragrance of medium strength. The compact, bushy growth makes this rose ideal for borders or it would be a great choice for hedging. We are honoured to name this after Her Royal Highness, the Princess Royal who is patron of Riding for the Disabled. The charity offers opportunities for therapy, achievement and enjoyment to people with disabilities. 90 x 60cm/3 x 2ft. 2010.

Princess Anne, a very new variety, it will create an impressive focal point in any border with its long flowering season and large flowers

***St. Alban** is
a beautiful rose at all
stages, from globular bud
to shallow cup filled with
numerous petals*

St. Alban (*Auschestnut*) As the blooms open, we have a lovely rounded globular bud, within which we can catch glimpses of numerous folded petals. Gradually they unfurl until we have an attractive shallow cup filled with numerous petals. The colour starts as a rich yellow, gradually tending towards a softer yellow. It has a pleasing fresh scent that is hard to define but has been described as similar to the fragrance we experience when we walk into a florist's shop. This is not a very formal flower — just a pretty arrangement of petals. The growth is of the kind we so much favour in the Leander group — a strong shrub, holding its numerous flowers nicely on arching branches. There is plentiful luxurious foliage. We named this rose in honour of the Royal National Rose Society, founded in 1876 and the first Society of its kind. Over the years, it has been at the centre of all matters to do with roses and has done much good work. 1.2 × 1.1m / 4 × 3½ft. 2003.

St. Cecilia (*Ausmit*) This variety bears medium-sized flowers of distinctly cupped, incurved formation and pale buff-apricot colouring, which can vary a little according to the season. These are held well apart in open sprays, nodding nicely on the stem. They have a strong and unusual fragrance of English Rose myrrh character, with hints of lemon and almond blossom. The growth is quite short and rather upright, making this an excellent rose for a small garden. St. Cecilia is the patron saint of music and musicians. 90×80cm / $3 \times 2\frac{1}{2}$ft. 1987.

St. Cecilia, being quite short and rather upright, makes an excellent rose for a small garden

113

*We have found that **Sir John Betjeman** is particularly good in a container where the strongly coloured flowers make a strong statement*

Sir John Betjeman (*Ausencart*) A rose of more modern character than most English Roses. The flowers start as small buds opening to full petalled, wide open rosettes of a bright, deep pink. As the flower ages the bloom becomes dome shaped while the colour—unusually for the English Roses—gradually intensifies. The flowers are about 7.5cm/3in across and are produced extremely freely and indeed is one of the most free flowering of all English Roses. They have a light, rather 'green' fragrance. A healthy and very bushy shrub of medium size with a slightly arching habit. With its bright colouration this would

be a good choice to create some contrast in a border of other roses of softer colouring. It could also be used in a more formal bedding scheme and is excellent in a large container. Altogether, a strong and healthy shrub that will grow well even in less than ideal conditions. The John Betjeman Society asked us to name this rose after the well-known poet. Sir John Betjeman was a writer, journalist and broadcaster. He also opened people's eyes to the value of the buildings and landscape around them. He was born just over 100 years ago. 100 x 75cm/3.5 x 2.5ft.

Strawberry Hill (*Ausrimini*) 'Strawberry Hill' bears medium sized, pure rose pink, cupped rosettes of superb quality; the colour gradually paling to a lighter pink at the edges — eventually exposing a few yellow stamens at the centre: beautiful at all stages. It has a particularly fine myrrh fragrance with a hint of lemon. Its growth is tall, vigorous and rather informal. It is slightly arching, with healthy and glossy, dark green leaves. This is a good rose for a position to the rear of a mixed border, or for a border of Shrub Roses. It will also make a good climber to 2.5m/8ft. Strawberry Hill is a beautiful house at Twickenham, built in the style of the Gothic revival, by the first British Prime Minister, Horace Walpole. He also laid out a fine garden which is being restored. 120cm x 120cm/4 x 4ft. 2006.

Summer Song (*Austango*) A rose of a lovely shade of burnt orange; such colours are not easy to come by and 'Summer Song' is therefore a valuable addition to our collection. The flowers start as rounded buds, opening to full cups with small glowing petals, arranged rather informally within a perfect ring of outer petals. They have a strong mixed scent, which our fragrance expert tells us is 'like walking into a florist's shop: hints of chrysanthemum leaves, ripe banana and tea'. It forms a bushy, upright shrub that might be pruned lower if required for bedding. $120 \times 90cm/4 \times 3ft$. 2005.

*Above, **Teasing Georgia** bears flowers of a crisp, cupped rosette formation; growth is tall and strong, without being stiff, making this rose ideal for a mixed border or for combining with other shrub roses*

*Facing page, **The Alnwick Rose** bears deeply cupped blooms that open to reveal crinkled petals, born on an upright shrub that is quite broad in growth and exceptionally vigorous*

Teasing Georgia (*Ausbaker*) One of the best and most beautiful members of the Leander group, the growth of 'Teasing Georgia' is tall and strong, without being stiff. Its plentiful foliage is dark, glossy and disease resistant. The flowers are of a particularly attractive formation: a crisp, cupped rosette. The colour is a rich, glowing yellow. They are held elegantly upon the branch and have a particularly fine Tea Rose fragrance. A refined and beautiful rose. Named for Ulrich Meyer, after his wife Georgia, both of whom are well-known media personalities in Germany. 90 × 110cm / 3 × 3½ft. It also makes an excellent climber of some 1.8–2.5m / 6–8ft in height. 1998.

The Alnwick Rose (*Ausgrab*) This is an upright shrub that is quite broad in growth and exceptionally vigorous, with plentiful, glossy, disease-free foliage. The flowers are a glowing medium pink, the colour deepening towards the centre and attractively cupped with numerous small petals within; the pistils provide a small yellow eye at the centre. There is a lovely Old Rose fragrance with just a hint of raspberry. If you want a good, reliable shrub of the Leander Group, it would be hard to beat this rose. We named it for the Duke and Duchess of Northumberland, who have made a magnificent 5 hectare / 12 acre garden at Alnwick Castle in Northumberland with a very large rose garden that includes many of our English Roses. 120 × 80cm / 4 × 2½ft. 2001.

__The Ingenious Mr Fairchild__ has very large flowers that are borne on a vigorous, arching shrub

The Ingenious Mr Fairchild (*Austijus*) We are always keen to develop large, peony-like roses with good shrubby growth. 'Golden Celebration' and 'Brother Cadfael' are good examples of such roses—and this is another. The flowers of 'The Ingenious Mr Fairchild' are in the form of deep cups filled with crisp, upstanding petals. The colour on the inside of the petals is a deep pink touched with lilac; the outside is of a paler shade. Looking at the bloom in more detail, one can see that the edges are an even deeper pink, giving a most delightful fringed effect—particularly in the earlier stages. It has a strong and deliciously fruity rose fragrance, with aspects of raspberry, peach and a hint of mint. The growth is ideal with spreading, arching branches building up into a well-rounded, mounding shrub, with its flowers nicely poised. It is very healthy. Named after Thomas Fairchild, a nurseryman of London and Fellow of the Royal Society, who made the first recorded flower hybrid in Europe in 1720. This was a cross between a Sweet William and a carnation, which became known as 'Fairchild's Mule'. We have to thank Michael Leapman for the name, which was the title of his biography of Thomas Fairchild. 1.2 × 1.1m / 4 × 3½ft. 2003.

William Morris (*Austir*) A tall shrub with attractive, rather arching growth and glossy foliage. The flowers are a lovely glowing apricot pink and of formal rosette shape. It is of the group which includes 'Geoff Hamilton', 'Leander' and 'A Shropshire Lad' and like them is extremely hardy and reliable, making it an ideal rose for further back in the border, where it will withstand competition better than most. It has a strong fragrance, which is difficult to describe but is nonetheless pleasing. Excellent repeat-flowering, especially for a shrub of its size. Good disease-resistance. Named to commemorate the centenary of the founding of the University of East London. $120 \times 90\text{cm} / 4 \times 3\text{ft}$. It also makes a good climber of some $2.4\text{m} / 8\text{ft}$. 1998.

Yellow Charles Austin (*Ausling*) A yellow sport of 'Charles Austin', which shares all its qualities and, other than colour, is exactly the same. 1981.

William Morris, a tall shrub bearing formal, rosette-shaped flowers, is an ideal rose for further back in the border, where it will withstand competition better than most

121

English Musk Roses

The English Musk Roses were bred by crossing our original Old Rose Hybrids with Noisette Roses. Like the Noisettes, they are lighter both in flower and growth than the previous two groups; the whole effect being one of daintiness and charm. Their colours, too, have a softness that is most appealing in a rose, with fresh pinks, blushes, soft yellows and shades of apricot and peach. The Musk Rose fragrance is unfortunately missing except in a few varieties; nonetheless, nearly all the other fragrances are to be found in these roses, sometimes mingled with the Musk scent.

Anne Boleyn (*Ausecret*) An exceptionally free-flowering variety that is quite short but widely spreading, with attractively arching growth which is almost completely free of disease. The flowers are of neat rosette shape, soft pink in colour and borne in quite large sprays—the individual blooms being produced in succession with remarkable continuity. There is only a light scent. The whole impression of this rose is one of pleasing freshness. A useful and healthy, reliable shrub. Named after the second of Henry VIII's six wives. 1 × 1.2m / 3 × 4ft. 1999.

Blythe Spirit (*Auschool*) This rose produces its flowers in sprays. The individual flowers are quite small, of cupped shape and a nice soft yellow, fading to pale lemon. They have a light Musk fragrance with a hint of myrrh. The growth is medium in height and it develops into a bushy shrub which mingles well with other plants. Its foliage is small and is, we believe, completely resistant to disease. An ideal border plant. Named after Noel Coward's play. 1.2 × 1.2m / 4 × 4ft. 1999.

*Facing page, **Anne Boleyn** is exceptionally free flowering, quite short but widely spreading and almost completely free of disease*

*Below, **Blythe Spirit** is an ideal border plant, developing into a bushy shrub that mingles well with other plants, and producing its cup-shaped flowers in sprays*

***Buttercup**, an excellent garden shrub, it is very tough and provides strong colour and delicious fragrance over a very long season*

Buttercup (*Ausband*) Numerous, small cupped flowers of pure golden-yellow, held in open sprays. The effect is that of a mass of rather large buttercups—a superb display that is repeated throughout the summer. It has smooth, light green foliage. It will form a fine garden shrub that is very reliable and almost completely resistant to disease. An ideal rose for the mixed border where, with its light airy growth, it associates well with other plants. There is often a particularly good display in late summer. A strong, delicious scent that is difficult to describe but is reminiscent of orange blossom and just occasionally of cocoa powder! $1.2 \times 1m / 4 \times 3ft$. 1998.

Cariad (*Auspanier*) A large, airy shrub with dainty, grey-green foliage. The flowers, which are held on thin, wiry stems, are a soft rose pink and are semi-double in form. They open to provide us with an almost camellia-like bloom which is most pleasing. Early in the season the fragrance is myrrh with a touch of tea at the bud stage, becoming a spicy musk when open. Later in the season the musky scent of the stamens is more in evidence, with elements of orange peel and almonds. An ideal garden shrub that will mingle naturally with other plants in the mixed border. It has excellent resistance to disease. The name 'Cariad' is Welsh for 'Love'. 130 x 100cm/4½ x 3½ft. 2010.

Cariad is an interesting variety in that the flowers change in character through the season, they start very double but become more semi double later in the year

Charlotte, bushy and vigorous, builds up to a small, well-filled shrub bearing cup-shaped flowers filled with twisted petals

Charlotte (*Auspoly*) This variety is often compared to 'Graham Thomas', although it is not yet so well known. Its colour is somewhat less intense—a lovely soft yellow. The flower is cup shaped and filled with beautifully arranged, twisted petals. They have a strong Tea Rose fragrance. Its growth is bushy and vigorous and builds up to a small, well-filled shrub. All in all, one of our best yellow roses. Although this rose was introduced before my granddaughter Charlotte was born, I have since dedicated it to her. 90 × 80cm / 3 × 2½ft. 1993.

Claire Austin, with large, rosette-shaped flowers, is robust and free flowering and forms a fine, rounded shrub of dense growth

Claire Austin (*Ausprior*) There is something a little special about white roses — they are all purity and light — and yet really good white roses are rare among English Roses and Hybrid Tea Roses alike. This is because white roses are very difficult to breed. 'Claire Austin' bears pleasingly cupped buds of a pale lemon shade which gradually open to form large, creamy-white flowers of typical English Musk delicacy; their petals are perfectly arranged in concentric circles, with a few more loosely arranged in the centre. They have a strong fragrance based on myrrh with dashes of meadowsweet, vanilla and heliotrope. It forms an elegant, arching shrub with plentiful, medium green foliage. Strong and particularly healthy it can either be grown as a tall shrub about 140cm/4.5ft tall by 90cm/3ft wide or an excellent climber to 2.5m/8ft. Claire Austin is my daughter. She has a nursery which specialises in hardy plants, including the country's finest collection of irises, peonies and day lilies. 2007.

Comte de Champagne (*Ausfo*) This is an interesting rose and is, in many ways, unique. The flowers are soft yellow at first—becoming pale yellow and even paler on the outside of the petals—gradually opening to form a perfect open cup of medium to large size. There is a 'mop' of deep yellow stamens; the whole providing a pleasing range of colour on the bush at one time. A delicious honey and Musk fragrance complements the flower to perfection. It is a rose of rather lax, spreading growth yet bushy, producing its flowers on

slender stems. It is healthy and free-flowering. This variety was named after Taittinger's finest champagne. The president of Taittinger, M. Claude Taittinger, lives in a château built by Thibaut IV, Count of Champagne and Brie, who brought *R. gallica* var. *officinalis* (the Apothecary's Rose) from Damascus on his return to France from the 7th Crusade in 1250. The Count was a great lover of roses and wrote about them in his poetry. 1.2 x 1.0m/4 x 3½ft. 2001.

Comte de Champagne, *in many ways a unique rose, providing a range of flower colour that is perfectly complemented by a delicious honey and Musk fragrance*

*Above, **Crocus Rose**, with large, rosette-shaped flowers, is robust and free-flowering and forms a fine, rounded shrub of dense growth*

*Facing page, **Evelyn** has some of the most magnificent individual blooms of any rose, it is particularly good in Mediterranean-type climates*

Crocus Rose (*Ausquest*) A robust and free-flowering rose, bearing large, rosette-shaped flowers that are cupped at first; the petals later reflexing. The colour is soft apricot, paling to cream on the outer petals. The flowers are produced very freely, in large clusters elegantly poised on the end of slightly arching stems. They have a light Tea Rose fragrance. Like 'Anne Boleyn', which is of similar breeding, it forms a fine, rounded shrub of dense growth and it, too, is very free from disease. Named for the Crocus Trust, which was set up to help sufferers affected by colorectal cancer. 120 × 90cm / 4 × 3ft. 2000.

Evelyn (*Aussaucer*) Particularly large, apricot and pink flowers of shallow, saucer-like formation with numerous petals which gradually recurve to form a rosette shape. They have a wonderful fragrance, similar in style to an Old Rose but with a sumptuous fruity note reminiscent of fresh peaches and apricot. This is a beautiful and quite startling rose, though not quite so reliable as we would like it to be, being somewhat subject to disease—although it does remarkably well in countries with a warm climate and indeed makes a wonderful climber to 2m/6ft. The growth is quite short and upright, making it useful for smaller gardens. It has typical, light green Musk Rose foliage. It was named on behalf of the perfumers, Crabtree & Evelyn. 90 × 80cm / 3 × 2½ft. 1991.

Francine Austin
will create a frothy mass
of glistening white flowers

Francine Austin (*Ausram*) A medium-sized shrub of spreading growth, bearing sprays of small, pure white, pompon flowers. As such, it is not truly an English Rose. I would, however, prefer to keep it here, as it has much of the appearance and refinement of the first Noisette Roses. The flowers are held well apart from each other on thin, wiry stems in dainty sprays. It blooms freely and continuously, its long branches wreathed with white, providing a lovely picture. Its leaves are pale green with numerous small leaflets. It is named after my daughter-in-law. 90–120cm / 3–4ft and as much across. 1988.

Graham Thomas (*Ausmas*) One of the best-known and most widely grown of the English Roses; indeed, it has much of the beauty and character of the Noisette Roses at their best. It is probably one of the most widely grown of all roses over the last twenty years or so. It has flowers of the richest and purest deep yellow, a shade which would be difficult to match in any other rose and is hard to

equal even among Modern Roses. The flowers are of medium size and deeply cupped at first, opening to form a beautiful cupped rosette, the petals mingling attractively within. They have a lovely, strong Tea Rose fragrance. The growth is very strong, breaking freely at almost every joint as well as at the base to produce further flowers. The leaves are smooth and of light green colouring. If we look for faults, we might say that the growth is a little too upright and narrow at the base but, as its namesake remarked: 'Too upright for what?' The late Graham Stuart Thomas, who chose this variety to bear his name, was the prime mover in the reintroduction of the Old Roses. He was a frequent visitor to our nursery and may be said to have paved the way for the development of the English Roses. James Mason Award 2000. In 2009 it was voted the World's Favourite Rose by the World Federation of Rose Societies. 120×90cm / 4×3ft. 1983.

'Graham Thomas' is equally suitable for growing as a climber, particularly on a wall where it can reach 3m / 10ft.

Graham Thomas, one of the best-known of the English Roses, has much of the beauty and character of the Noisette Roses at their best and is equally good in the mixed border and as a climber

***Heritage** produces flowers in sprays on smooth stems with few thorns*

Heritage (*Ausblush*) With 'Graham Thomas', this was one of the first English Roses of the Noisette group and it has all the delicate beauty we would expect of such a rose. Its flowers are of medium size and of a most perfect cupped formation. Their colour is a soft blush pink and the petals within the cup are each placed with exquisite perfection, giving it a shell-like beauty. The flowers are produced in small—and occasionally large—sprays. There is a lovely fragrance which has been described as having overtones of fruit, honey and carnation on a myrrh background. The stems are smooth with few thorns and typical, pointed Hybrid Musk Rose foliage. In growth and leaf 'Heritage' has much in common with the rose 'Graham Thomas', which shares the same parentage. It forms a nice, shapely rounded shrub, breaking freely along the stem to produce further flowers. If it has a fault, it is that it has a tendency to disease and needs to be sprayed. $1.2 \times 1.2m / 4 \times 4ft$. 1984.

Jayne Austin (*Ausbreak*) This is truly a beautiful rose. The flowers are shallowly cupped at first, later becoming rosette shaped. They are yellow, tending a little towards apricot—the outer petals being paler—and their petals have the lovely silky sheen that we find in the Noisette Roses and their descendants. The growth of this rose is slender and upright—perhaps a little too much so—a tendency it owes to its parent, 'Graham Thomas'. The leaves are plentiful and pale green. It has a wonderful Tea Rose fragrance. Named after my daughter-in-law. 1.1m / $3\frac{1}{2}$ ft. 1990.

Jayne Austin bears beautiful, shallowly cupped flowers that have a strong Tea fragrance

Kew Gardens is most unusual in the rose world as it is completely thornless—even the underside of the leaf is prickle free

Kew Gardens (*Ausfence*) This is not truly an English Rose but we include it here for convenience as it has connections with our Musk Hybrids. The flowers, which are small and single, are held in very large heads rather like a hydrangea and produced almost continuously from early summer through to the end of the season. The young buds are soft apricot opening to pure white, with a hint of soft lemon behind the stamens. The flowers are followed by small red hips which should be removed to encourage repeat flowering. It is extremely healthy and completely thornless—a most unusual thing among roses. It has a bushy

but rather upright habit of growth, making it ideal for the back of a mixed border. A group of two or three or more bushes will provide a mass of white as though they were covered with snow. This rose is particularly suitable for forming a magnificent impenetrable flowering hedge. We named this rose in celebration of the 250th anniversary of Kew Gardens. We replanted the rose garden behind the famous Palm House, returning it to the layout of 1848 and filling it with a wonderful mixture of English Roses, Old Roses and other shrub roses. 150 x 90cm/5 x 3ft. 2009.

Lady Emma Hamilton (*Ausbrother*) The buds of this variety are dark red with dashes of orange. They open to form an incurving, cup-shaped flower of apricot-orange. The fully open flowers are a lovely mixture of rich tangerine-orange on the inside of the petals, while the outer petals are an orange-yellow; the whole is set off by dark, bronzy-green foliage which becomes dark green with age. The unusual range of colour for an English Rose is useful for creating a little excitement in the border. There is a strong and delicious fruity fragrance, with hints of pear, grape and citrus fruits. A fairly upright, rather bushy shrub of medium height, producing its flowers freely. Very healthy. Named to commemorate the 200th Anniversary of the Battle of Trafalgar. 120 × 90cm / 4 × 3ft. 2005.

Lichfield Angel (*Ausrelate*) The flowers of this rose commence as charming little peachy pink cups, gradually opening to form neatly cupped rosettes, each with a with a perfect ring of creamy-apricot waxy petals enclosing numerous smaller petals. Eventually the petals turn back to form a domed, creamy-white flower. It is particularly free flowering, the overall effect in the mass being almost pure white. 'Lichfield Angel' will form a vigorous, rounded shrub which,

*Facing page, **Lady Emma Hamilton**, a wonderful and rather different English Rose with strongly coloured flowers that are set off by the dark, bronze-coloured leaves*

*Below, **Lichfield Angel** shows the pristine perfection of the English Musks at their best*

Lucetta has a simple but very lovely bloom and is seldom out of flower

with its blooms nodding attractively on the branch, will make a fine sight. It will be very useful in a border, as it will go well with all other colours and will act as an intermediary between pinks and yellows. The fragrance is generally light but is strongly clove at one stage. 'The Lichfield Angel' is a limestone sculptured panel dating from the 8th century which was discovered in Lichfield Cathedral. It depicts St. Chad and still bears the remnants of Saxon paint. 120 x 90cm/4 ft x 3ft. 2006.

Lucetta (*Ausemi*) Very large, wide open and flat, semi-double, saucer-like flowers of a soft blush-pink, becoming paler with age, with a large boss of stamens. This is a particularly good shrub, healthy and strong growing, to about 1.5m/5ft in height and as much across, with long, arching branches. The large blooms are nicely poised and contrast well with its ample, dark green foliage. It is seldom without flowers and is in every way tough and reliable. Fragrant. 1983.

Maid Marion (*Austobias*) 'Maid Marion' at its best produces some of the most superbly formed flowers we have seen. The buds start as rounded cups with larger outer petals, enclosing numerous smaller petals within. These open to the most perfect rosette-shaped flowers in the form of a saucer; the outer petals forming a perfectly rounded rim. Their colour is a clear rose pink. The growth is relatively upright but quite bushy and compact. Initially the fragrance is a soft myrrh—as the flower ages it becomes more fruity with a distinct clove character. 'Maid Marion' was the companion of the mythical hero 'Robin Hood of Sherwood Forest'. 90 x 90cm/3ft x 3ft. 2010.

Maid Marion has some of the most perfectly formed blooms of any English Rose

Marinette (*Auscam*) The flowers of this rose start as very long, pencil-thin buds that unfold to become wide, flat, semi-double flowers of palest pink, with a fine bunch of golden stamens. They are held on slender stems, which completes the effect of lightness and grace. They have a soft and pleasing fragrance. The growth is rounded and well balanced; the flowers and shrub as a whole mixing easily with other plants. This rose is named for Marina Berry, known to her friends as Marinette. Not a typical English Rose, but beautiful nonetheless. 1.2m / 4ft. 1995.

Molineux (*Ausmol*) Of all the English Roses this is, perhaps, the best for bedding, although it is also useful at the front of a border. It flowers with exceptional freedom and continuity, has short, even, upright growth and is exceptionally free from disease. Its flowers are a rich, pure yellow and in the

*The flowers of **Marinette** go through three very distinct phases, each very beautiful in its own right*

form of a neat rosette. They have a good Tea Rose fragrance with a musky background. Not quite the 'typical' English Rose, in that it lacks that indefinable Old Rose character, but it is nonetheless an exceptionally good rose. Named for the Wolverhampton Wanderers Football Club, 'Molineux' being the name of their ground. 90cm / 3ft. 1994.

Mortimer Sackler (*Ausorts*) This rose is something a little different. The flowers are dainty, about 7cm / 3in across, and borne on slender, upright stems with very few thorns. They open to shallow, dainty cups of soft pink, paling a little on the outer petals. As they mature, they take on a rather star-like formation, gradually exposing golden stamens. There is a lovely fragrance: Old Rose with a delicious hint of fruit. The growth is tall and rigidly upright and perhaps a little bare at the base of its branches, making it really only suitable for the back of the border. The stems and leaves are red at first, gradually becoming dark green. This rose was auctioned by the National Trust to raise funds for their gardens. It was bought by Mrs Sackler for her husband Mortimer's birthday. 1.4×1.1m / $4\frac{1}{2} \times 3\frac{1}{2}$ft. 2002.

*Facing page, **Molineux** flowers with exceptional freedom and continuity and, of all the English Roses, is the best for bedding and for the front of a border*

*Below, **Mortimer Sackler** bears dainty, cup-shaped flowers on slender stems with very few thorns*

*Below, **Pegasus**, particularly good as a cut flower, it also has a strong Tea Rose fragrance*

*Facing page, The blooms of **Perdita** start off quite pointed and Hybrid Tea-like but then open out fully to a very full rosette*

Pegasus (*Ausmoon*) This rose stands a little apart from other English Roses in that it has flowers that have petals of a rather more than usually substantial and waxy quality. They are of a pleasing formality, in the form of a full rosette shape and a rich apricot-yellow. They have a strong Tea Rose fragrance. The growth is particularly arching in character, which gives it an added attraction, and the foliage is of a rather Hybrid Tea appearance. It is a particularly good rose as a cut flower, which will last well in water. It was named after the winged horse of Greek mythology, rather appropriately, for Riding for the Disabled, a charity that gives much pleasure to many disabled children. 90×110cm/$3 \times 3\frac{1}{2}$ft. 1995.

Perdita (*Ausperd*) A good small shrub with bushy, slightly arching growth to about 1.1m/$3\frac{1}{2}$ft, constantly shooting from the base and providing continuity of bloom. The flowers are fully double, of medium size, delicate apricot-blush in colour and of shallowly dished, rather cupped formation. It has ample, dark green, foliage and red-brown stems. The fragrance is strongly of myrrh with a hint of Tea Rose, and it was awarded the Royal National Rose Society's Henry Edland Medal for fragrance in 1984. Named after the character in Shakespeare's *The Winter's Tale*. 1983.

*Facing page, **Port Sunlight** bears flowers of rosette formation, with a strong Tea Rose fragrance, and is particularly good as a cut flower*

*Above, **Queen of Sweden** is a small-flowered rose whose growth is tough and reliable*

Port Sunlight (*Auslofty*) This rose bears medium sized flowers of rich apricot colouring. They are of flat rosette shape and slightly quartered at the centre; the outer petals falling back a little and becoming paler. They have a rich Tea fragrance. The foliage and young stems are bronzy-red at first, becoming a fairly dark green. The growth is vigorous and rather upright, about 150cm/5ft in height by 1.0m/3.5ft across, making it ideal for the back of a mixed border where it will compete well with other plants. It is very resistant to disease. All in all, a very good, reliable variety. It is named after the model village in the Wirral built by William Hesketh Lever, where they have a beautiful garden of English Roses. 2007.

Queen of Sweden (*Austiger*) The flowers of a rose do not have to be large to be beautiful; there is, in fact, something appealing about small-flowered roses and often their growth is tough and reliable. 'Queen of Sweden' is such a rose. It has small to medium-sized flowers which are prettily cupped and incurved at first, gradually opening out to a neat rosette. They start a glowing apricot-pink, later becoming a lovely soft Alba Rose pink which gradually pales on the outer petals. They have a light to medium myrrh fragrance. The growth is rather rigid, a fact that only seems to add to its beauty. The foliage is typically Musk Rose and very disease-resistant. A charming little rose that grows in popularity each year. Named in celebration of the 350th anniversary of the Treaty of Friendship and Commerce between Queen Christina of Sweden and Oliver Cromwell of Great Britain in 1654. 110 × 80cm/3½ × 2½ft. 2004.

Facing page, **Rose of Picardy** *produces single red blooms with exceptional freedom, giving a display that can be seen across the garden*

Below, **Scepter'd Isle** *is suitable for bedding or for a place at the front of the border, its deeply cupped flowers having a very strong myrrh fragrance*

Rose of Picardy (*Ausfudge*) Until we introduced 'Rose of Picardy' we had no single red roses. It has single, bright scarlet-crimson flowers of exceptional daintiness. They are about 7cm / 3in. across with contrasting golden stamens and they have a light, fruity fragrance. It blooms with exceptional freedom, giving a display that can be seen across the garden. The flowers are followed by numerous red hips, which have their own beauty. However, as is usually the case, if you have hips you do not have many flowers, so for greater cropping later in the season it is necessary to remove these hips. We felt that, for obvious reasons, this poppy-like rose was suitable to bear this very important name and so, with our French friends very much in mind, it was named to celebrate the Entente Cordiale between Britain and France. 1.2m / 4ft. 2004.

Scepter'd Isle (*Ausland*) This charming little rose is similar to 'Heritage' but, being shorter, more upright and particularly free flowering, is suitable for bedding or for a place at the front of the border. Its flowers are medium sized and deeply cupped. Their colour is a lovely soft pink that pales on the outside of the petals. There is a very strong myrrh fragrance. The stems and leaves are light green—similar to those of 'Heritage'—showing signs of Musk Rose ancestry. The name is taken from John of Gaunt's speech, expressing his love for England in Shakespeare's *Richard II*. 90cm / 3ft. 1996.

*Above, **Sweet Juliet**, a tough rose with shallowly cupped flowers of superb quality and a strong lemon fragrance*

*Facing page, **Tea Clipper**, suitably for a rose of this name, has a Tea scent, with hints of fruit and myrrh*

Sweet Juliet (*Ausleap*) This variety is very similar to 'Jayne Austin', with flowers of the same superb quality. They are medium sized, of shallowly cupped shape and apricot-yellow in colour, paling towards the edges. There is a strong Tea scent which develops a lemon character as the flower matures. It requires harder pruning than most English Roses, otherwise the plant will become ungainly and the flowers small. Named for the heroine of Shakespeare's *Romeo and Juliet*. 110 × 90cm / 3½ × 3ft. 1989.

Tea Clipper (*Auscover*) Our wish is that English Roses should, unlike most Modern Roses, be as variable as possible in more than just colour; that each new variety should have its own unique character and beauty. 'Tea Clipper' is of a similar rich apricot to 'Grace' although in every other way it is a very different rose. The large flowers are of an informal rosette shape and nicely quartered, each with a button eye which is retained to the end. It forms a large, rather upright shrub with its flowers nodding on the branch. It is almost completely without thorns and is particularly healthy. Usually the fragrance is a lovely mix of tea, myrrh and fruit, although sometimes it is almost pure citrus. Named for the last and finest of the sailing ships to mark the centenary of the death of Frederick Horniman whose collection of fascinating objects from around the world is housed in the Horniman Museum. 120 x 90cm/4 x 3ft.

Above, **The Generous Gardener** *has beautifully formed flowers and arching growth with polished dark green foliage*

Facing page, **The Pilgrim** *has flowers with a softness of character rare among yellow roses, soft green foliage and a fragrance that perfectly combines tea and myrrh*

The Generous Gardener (*Ausdrawn*) A rose of delicate charm, its flowers being beautifully formed; their colour is a soft glowing pink at the centre, shading to palest pink on the outer petals. When the petals open they expose numerous stamens, providing an almost water lily-like effect. It has strong, elegantly arching growth with polished dark green foliage. This rose is most effective when placed at the back of a border, looking over other plants. Like all our recent varieties, this rose is highly disease-resistant. It has a delicious fragrance with aspects of Old Rose, Musk and myrrh. 'The Generous Gardener' was named to commemorate the seventy-fifth anniversary of the National Gardens Scheme which has, over the years, made it possible for us all to see many beautiful gardens. 1.5 × 1.2m / 5 × 4ft. It is particularly lovely as a climber. 2002.

The Pilgrim (*Auswalker*) The flowers of this variety are particularly beautiful, having a softness of character that is rare among yellow roses. Perhaps this is due to its Musk Rose background. Its blooms are pale yellow, quite large and beautifully formed in the shape of a shallowly cupped rosette. Their fragrance is a perfect balance between that of a Tea Rose and English myrrh. It will form a nice shrub of medium to large size, with soft green foliage that is very healthy and blends perfectly with the flowers. It is also a very good climber. Named after the pilgrims of Chaucer's *The Canterbury Tales*. 1.2m / 4ft. 1991.

*Above, **The Shepherdess** is a variety of quiet unassuming beauty but one that is well worth incorporating into the garden*

*Facing page, the blooms of **The Wedgwood Rose** are some of the most beautiful to be found in the English Roses. It is very much more of a climber than a shrub rose*

The Shepherdess (*Austwist*) This rose has cupped flowers of a pleasing apricot-pink. They have a slightly waxy appearance that we often find in roses of the English Musk Group. Within the cup we see attractively folded petals. The blooms are of medium size and have a lovely fruity fragrance with hints of lemon. The growth is not tall but vigorous and upright. The foliage is large for an English Musk. Named after a character in Sir Philip Sidney's 16th-century prose romance, *The Arcadia.* 90 × 60cm / 3 × 2ft. 2005.

The Wedgwood Rose (*Ausjosiah*) The individual flowers of this rose are among the most beautiful we have ever bred. This variety is also, insofar as we can tell, almost completely free of disease — something that can be said of only a very few roses. The blooms are of medium to large size and have petals of a delicate, almost gossamer-like quality; the colour being a soft rose pink — all this adding up to a charming Old Rose effect. They have a lovely fruity fragrance on the outer petals, with a clove-like scent at the centre. The growth is exceptionally vigorous, sending up many shoots from the base and forming a large, rampant shrub perhaps 1.5m/5ft tall and across but is perhaps better grown as a climber to 3m/10ft. Its ample foliage is dark green and glossy. It was named for Wedgwood, who celebrated their 250th anniversary in 2009. Josiah Wedgwood, the 'Father of English Potters', founded the company in 1759. 2009.

Wildeve bears a mass of flowers all along its arching branches

Wildeve (*Ausbonny*) A robust and healthy rose, bearing a mass of flowers all the way along its arching branches, to form a wide, mounding shrub. The buds are blush-pink at first, opening to fully double, rosette-shaped flowers that are pink with a touch of apricot at the centre, fading to white at the edges. They are of medium size, and slightly quartered at the centre. It has a pleasing, fresh fragrance of medium strength. The foliage is small, clean, plentiful and free from disease. We would expect it to do well in a less than perfect position, although it is worth something better. All in all, a fine example of an English Musk Rose. 110 × 110cm / $3\frac{1}{2}$ × $3\frac{1}{2}$ ft. 2003.

*A particularly tough and healthy rose, **Wisley 2008** is ideal for mixed borders and as a hedge*

Wisley 2008 (*Ausbreeze*) This is a rose of exceptional delicacy and charm bearing some resemblance to the old Alba Roses. The flowers are shallowly cupped and about 7.5cm/3in across; the petals arranged in a most perfect rosette formation — their colour being a very pure soft pink; the outer petals paling a little towards the edge. It bears some resemblance to an old Alba Rose such as 'Queen of Denmark'. The growth is tall and elegantly arching, producing its flowers along the stems and building up into a fine, vigorous shrub of 1.5m/5ft in height. There is a delightful, fresh, fruity fragrance with hints of raspberries and Tea. It is a good choice for both formal and informal areas of the garden and also, perhaps, for a hedge. Named for the famous Royal Horticultural Society Gardens at Wisley where many English Roses are planted. 2008.

English Alba Rose Hybrids

These are the most recent roses of the English Rose family and a little way removed from the other groups. The difference lies in their almost wild rose growth, which means they associate easily with other plants and makes them suitable not only for more formal planting, but also for the wilder areas of the garden. Their breeding originates in crosses between Alba Roses and other English Roses. They usually have light and airy growth with foliage of a similar nature. Their colours at present are confined to shades of pink. The flowers are light and dainty and some gardeners regard this group as being among the most beautiful of roses. They are not yet quite so resistant to disease as we would like them to be — the lower leaves sometimes falling off to leave a bare stem — although this does not seem to be unsightly.

Ann (*Ausfete*) This is a single-flowered rose with just the occasional extra petal. Its colour is deep pink tinged with yellow at the centre, with a nice bunch of yellow stamens with red anthers. The flowers are beautifully poised, slightly drooping on the branch. The fragrance is delicate but pleasing. The growth is quite short but broad and the plant as a whole is a picture of simple daintiness. Named after Ann Saxby, one of our longest-serving employees, who has grown our roses for Chelsea Flower Show for many years. I think this is my favourite single English Rose. 90×80cm / $3 \times 2\frac{1}{2}$ft. 1997.

***Ann** is a picture of daintiness, the single flowers beautifully poised on the branch*

Cordelia (*Ausbottle*) Pretty, slender buds open into loosely petalled, semi-double flowers of a delightful shade of the purest rose pink. These are borne in large sprays, each bloom paling individually to provide a pleasing, mixed effect. The growth is dense and spreading, with the individual flowers held daintily above the foliage. Named after King Lear's youngest daughter in Shakespeare's play. 110 × 90cm / 3½ × 3ft. 2000.

***Cordelia** has loosely petalled, semi-double flowers held daintily above the foliage*

Scarborough Fair
bears cupped flowers that
open to reveal golden
stamens, and does so with
remarkable freedom and
continuity

Scarborough Fair (*Ausoran*) It is easy to be overwhelmed by the sheer size and weight of a flower. This rose is something quite different—its flowers are modest but charming. It is not unlike the beautiful 'Windflower' except that it is low and broad in growth, making it more suitable for a position where space is limited, or indeed for a place at the front of a border. The petals in the bud curl around to form a ball, which opens to a perfect little cupped flower of pure soft pink, eventually opening wide to reveal a blush pink flower of the utmost delicacy and a bunch of golden stamens. Charming at all stages. It flowers with remarkable freedom and continuity from June until the autumn. There is a delightful light to medium, fresh 'green' Old Rose fragrance, sometimes tending towards Musk. Very healthy, tough and reliable—as we might expect from its Alba antecedents. We have taken the name from the well-known medieval English folk song. $80 \times 60cm / 2\frac{1}{2} \times 2$ft. 2003.

Shropshire Lass was the foundation rose of the English Alba Hybrids

Shropshire Lass Just as 'Constance Spry' was the founding parent of the English Old Rose Hybrids, so 'Shropshire Lass' was the foundation rose of the English Alba Hybrids. It was the result of a cross between an old Hybrid Tea, 'Madame Butterfly', and the beautiful Alba, 'Madame Legras de Saint Germain'. It forms a large, strong shrub of some 2.5m/8ft in height and—like its parent—is extremely tough and disease-resistant. The flowers are blush white and almost single, 9 or 12cm/4 or 5in across, with a large boss of stamens. The fragrance is strong and delicious, with hints of myrrh. Unfortunately, being a first cross between a repeat-flowering and a non-repeat-flowering rose it is, itself, non-repeating; however, in compensation, it has enormous strength and freedom of flowering and it bears a wonderful crop of hips in the autumn. This rose is even better when grown as a climber, when it will reach considerable heights of 4–5m/12–15ft. 1968.

Skylark, altogether a very light and airy rose with delightful semi-double flowers and slender growth

Skylark (*Ausimple*) It is always our desire to bring as much variety of form, fragrance and growth as possible to our English Roses and this rose is a good example. The flowers are semi-double and of open, cupped shape with prominent stamens. The colour is deep pink at first, later paling slightly to lilac-pink. At the centre of the flower there is a small white area. There is a light but pleasing fragrance—Musk and Tea with clove and a hint of 'apple pie'! The growth is light and airy, building up into a natural, well-rounded shrub of 90cm/3 ft high by 60cm/2ft across. An ideal choice for planting amongst other shrubs or perennials towards the front of a mixed border. The name was suggested by Sister Elizabeth who remembers seeing and hearing a skylark when she first visited our Nursery. 2007.

*Facing page, **The Alexandra Rose** has flowers with a soft Musk fragrance that are produced in great abundance and repeat very well*

*Above, **The Lady's Blush** a charming variety that gives the overall impression of freshness and light*

The Alexandra Rose (*Ausday*) A dainty, single-flowered variety with flowers of rather less than medium size. These are a soft coppery pink that quickly fades to a blush pink, giving us a delightful mixed effect in the spray. They are produced in great abundance and repeat very well. There is a soft Musk fragrance. A shrub of elegant growth with the flowers held on twiggy stems. An excellent choice for the border or for a wild area, where it will have the advantage over other shrubs of producing flowers over a long season. Named for the Alexandra Rose Day, which raises money for a variety of charities. 1.2m/4ft. 1992.

The Lady's Blush (*Ausoscar*) A charming semi-double variety. The flowers start as elegant pointed buds and develop into rounded cups. Their colour is a pure soft pink with a creamy-white eye at the centre and often a white stripe. As with all semi-double roses, the central group of stamens is a very important feature. These are particularly fine; a beautiful soft yellow colour with highlights of golden-yellow pollen. At the point of attachment to the stamens there is a prominent red ring which accentuates the effect. The overall impression is of freshness and grace. This is a healthy variety, perfect for all types of borders. Especially effective when grown with annuals or perennials in a mixed border. A rose of dainty, natural beauty. It will grow into an attractive rounded bushy plant. Named for the 125th anniversary of *The Lady* magazine, which is the oldest weekly magazine for women. 120 x 90cm/4 x 3ft. 2010.

Windflower,
not unlike an herbaceous
anemone or windflower,
this is a rose for the border
or for wilder areas of
the garden

Windflower (*Auscross*) A dainty rose, holding its medium-sized blooms high up on wiry stems, giving it an appearance not unlike that of an herbaceous anemone or windflower. Pretty little buds open to loosely petalled, slightly cupped, soft pink flowers that are nicely poised on thin stems, providing a most beautiful, airy effect. They have an Old Rose fragrance with just a hint of apple and cinnamon. The foliage is of the true English Alba type, tending towards that of *Rosa canina*. This is very much a rose for the border or for the wilder areas of the garden, where it will associate well with other plants. For overall effect and almost wildflower beauty, both of flower and growth, this is one of the most beautiful English Roses. 120 × 90cm / 4 × 3ft. 1994.

English Roses Cultivation

When I am asked for my opinion on the cultivation of English Roses, I usually start by saying that this need not be arduous. If you do no more than work the soil to a reasonable tilth and then plant your roses, firming them in gently, you can be sure of reasonable results. If you then prune them each year to a height of about two-thirds, you will have good results every year. How good these will be depends, in some degree, on the soil being of at least average quality.

Having said this, if you are prepared to do a little more work, this will not only give you much better results, but also a great deal more satisfaction. The following notes are intended for those who wish to make the most of their roses. Before I go further, I should say that my advice is for gardeners in the British Isles and other temperate regions in the northern hemisphere. Gardeners in other climates will need to consult books on rose growing in their area.

Most ancestors of the garden rose are natives of more fertile areas of the world and it is worth giving them a prime position. However, even the poorest soils can be made suitable by adding generous quantities of humus. Again, roses will not thrive in a position where there is too much shade. Avoid any area that has overhanging trees. South-facing sites are entirely satisfactory. West-facing is no problem. East-facing sites are not very good and a north-facing site is not really suitable at all. The problem is not only a question of shade; roses do not like competition from the roots of trees and shrubs. It is better to plant well away from these.

Then there is the question of rose re-plant disease; it is certain that if a rose is planted in soil where roses have been before, they seldom thrive, even when the removed roses have been doing well. The simple answer to this is to move on and plant in fresh ground. Unfortunately this is not always possible—particularly in a carefully planned formal garden and in a position where you specifically desire to have roses. The choice in such cases is to either replace the soil with high quality new soil from a different area before planting the new ones or to treat the soil where they have been growing with ample quantities of humus and Root Grow.

Preparing the Soil

It is advisable to prepare the soil thoroughly before you plant. Dig to a depth of about 30cm/1ft. This should be done by trench digging: as you move the top soil, break up the sub-soil in the trench with a fork to give good drainage and enable the long tap roots to go down deep. Give the top soil a liberal dressing of either well-rotted compost or well-rotted manure. This should be carefully mixed with the soil. Alternatively, you may find it convenient to buy proprietary planting compost from your Garden Centre.

Planting

Planting of bare-rooted roses can be done at any time from autumn to late spring (mid October to the end of April in the UK). If you purchase container-grown roses, these can be planted at any time of year. In my opinion, bare-rooted roses are marginally superior to those grown in pots but in any case, after a year or two, there is likely to be very little difference.

Pruning

People are often baffled by the whole question of pruning. This is usually because they think it is more difficult than it really is. I believe it is as much an art as a craft. A lot depends on the end you wish to achieve. The following instructions on pruning should not be taken too literally. Much will depend on the size and even the shape of the shrub you require.

We have English Roses in the centre of our Renaissance Garden which are pruned much more severely than I suggest below and make the most beautiful small shrubs, whereas they could in another place be allowed to grow into much larger shrubs. Pruning may also depend, in some degree, on whether you require large individual flowers or a mass of smaller flowers. If you require the former, you will take away more wood; if you require the latter, you will leave more growth.

In the UK and elsewhere with relatively mild winters, pruning may be carried out at any time between the beginning of December and the end of March. Later pruning avoids any chance of the new shoots being caught by a late frost. I prefer earlier pruning for repeat-flowering roses, as they then get an earlier start, ensuring a longer season of flowering. It is always disappointing to see the last flush of bloom cut off by an early frost, but I would rather take this risk. In regions with cold winters, I would suggest it is better to delay pruning until spring growth is just starting.

The English Roses are a diverse group bred from a wide variety of different parents. This makes it difficult to lay down hard and fast rules for pruning. Since we have done our best to breed roses of natural, bushy or arching growth, it is important to encourage and retain this rather than change it by over-pruning. If the growth is naturally bushy, insofar as is possible, try to help the rose to express itself.

As a rule, it is usually best to first reduce the growth by one third. This may vary in accordance with the kind of shrub you require for any particular position. It is quite possible to prune a quite large English Rose very severely and get a quite small shrub. Having done the initial pruning, go over the plant again and cut back the short side shoots to about 8 or 10cm/3 or 4in. As the years go by, it will be necessary to occasionally take out dying and unproductive growth.

Removing Suckers

Most roses are grown on root stocks and from time to time these may send up their own shoots which are generally known as 'suckers'. It is vital that these should be removed as soon as possible; otherwise they will soon take over the whole plant. Cut them as hard back as you can. It is advisable to take a little bark of the stock as you do this, thus eliminating all possibilities of it shooting again from the same point.

Maintenance

Having completed the pruning of our roses, it is now necessary to consider the question of maintenance. By pruning time the soil will have become rather compacted and a light pricking over of the soil with a fork to a depth of 2 or 5cm/1 or 2in will help to aerate it. It also gives a chance to remove any weeds that may have appeared. At this time it will be desirable to give the soil a feed in the form of a long-term fertilizer. Such rose fertilizers are available and they are nearly all good.

This done, it is a good idea to lay down a mulch of rotted compost or farmyard manure. This is not essential, but there is nothing better you can do in order to provide a good show of blooms in the coming summer. It will keep the soil cool and retain moisture—and at the same time help the life in the soil and provide an additional source of nutrition. During the flowering season, further dressings of fertilizers can be given at intervals. These should be high in nitrogen and should be applied towards the end of a flush of bloom in order to encourage further growth and flowers for the next flush.

During the summer, dead-heading will be necessary. This will stop the formation of hips, which use up the energy of the plant, thus inhibiting further bloom. This also gives us the opportunity to tidy up the shrub generally. If a rose is single flowered, it will often produce decorative hips and you may prefer to retain these rather than have further bloom.

Watering

Watering is not essential in the British climate, but there can be no doubt that it will ensure much better flowering and continuity of flowering. Most garden plants flower only once in a season, but the rose has been bred to flower throughout the summer. It can do this well only if it is provided with moisture.

Diseases and Pests

Disease in roses is perhaps their greatest drawback as a garden plant, yet I do not think it is as bad as some people think. It is possible to grow roses without spraying, if they are scattered around the garden rather than planted close to each other. If you have a rose border or a rose garden it is almost always necessary to spray, unless you confine yourself to a rather restricted number of disease-free varieties. The more recent English Roses come into this category.

There are a number of excellent sprays on the market and they can be obtained from any garden centre. They should be used in accordance with the makers' instructions. Spraying should be done as soon as the disease appears and repeated at intervals throughout the summer.

There are four main diseases of roses:

Powdery Mildew This looks rather like a white powder. It is encouraged by dryness at the roots and so can be prevented by deep watering before the soil dries out. It is often variety specific.

Blackspot Usually occurs in midsummer (July or August in the UK) and spreads rapidly if not controlled. The spores only germinate if the leaves stay wet for at least seven hours when the weather is warm. Therefore, if you are watering, do so at a time when the leaves can dry out relatively quickly—usually in the morning. There is a great deal of variability in resistance between varieties although most have the potential to blackspot.

Rust This appears as bright orange and later black pustules on the undersides of the leaves and occasionally stems. It occurs in cool weather, early or more likely late in the season. It is more difficult to eradicate but spraying will at least hold it back.

Downy Mildew Is not so common as the other three and is rather hard to detect. One sure sign is when the leaves begin to drop prematurely. Downy mildew tends to occur when you have low night temperatures and high humidity in the day. Because of that, you tend to get it earlier and later in the season. It is a disease that is found only on certain varieties.

Insect pests are less of a problem than disease. They are easily controlled by spraying with a proprietary insecticide. Alternatively encourage as many beneficial insects into your garden as possible, they can be most effective.

The Life-Span of a Rose

Finally, there is the question of 'How long does a rose actually live?' This is rather like asking 'How long is a piece of string?' Some roses live for a very long time, as much as one hundred years or more.

However, there is no doubt that there comes a point when any rose will begin to deteriorate. There is often a gradual decline. Before this becomes too steep, it is probably best to dig the rose up and replace it. On the whole, it is repeat-flowering roses that tend to die earliest; they are under greater strain to produce flowers throughout the summer.

Glossary

Anther The part of the flower which produces pollen; the upper section of the stamen.

Arching shrub A shrub in which the long main branches bend down towards the soil, usually in a graceful manner.

Balled, balling The clinging together of petals due to damp, so that the bloom fails to open.

Bare-root roses Roses bought without soil, not in a container.

Basal shoot The strong main shoot that arises from the base of the rose.

Bicolour A rose bloom with two distinct shades of colour.

Boss The bunch of stamens at the centre of a flower.

Bract A modified leaf at the base of a flower stalk.

Break New growth from a branch.

Budding The usual method for the propagation of roses by the grafting of a leaf bud on to the neck of a root stock.

Bud-shaped flower I have coined this term to describe rose blooms that are in the form of a Hybrid Tea, i.e. flowers that are of high-centred bud formation and mainly beautiful in the bud (as opposed to those of Old Rose formation).

Bud Union The point where the rose stems join the root stock.

Bush I use this word to describe a closely pruned bedding rose, as for example a Hybrid Tea.

Bushy shrub A rose of dense, rounded growth.

Button Eye A button-like fold of petals in the centre of a rose bloom.

Calyx The green protective cover over the flower bud which opens into five sepals.

Cane A long rose stem, from the base of the plant, particularly as in a Rambling Rose.

Chromosomes Chains of linked genes contained in the cells of plants and animals.

Climbing Sport See Sport; the climbing form of this phenomenon.

Corymb A flower cluster that is flat-topped, or nearly so.

Cross See Hybrid.

Cultivar Plant raised or selected in cultivation.

Denomination The intellectual nomenclature recognised world wide under the auspices of plant breeders' rights and patents.

Die back The progressive dying back of a shoot from the tip.

Diploid A plant with two sets of chromosomes.

Flore Pleno Double flower.

Flush A period of blooming.

Gene A unit of heredity controlling inherited characteristics of a plant.

Genus, genera A group or groups of plants having common characteristics, e.g. *Rosa*.

Group The name for cultivars that have similar characteristics

Heeling-in Temporary planting of roses when conditions are not suitable for permanent planting.

Height The heights given for individual varieties are only approximate. Much will depend on soil, site, season and severity of pruning and geographic area. The breadth of a rose bush or shrub will usually be slightly less than the height and is the second quoted figure in the dimensions.

Hips, heps Seed pods of a rose.

Hybrid A rose resulting from crossing two different species or varieties.

Leaflets The individual section of a leaf.

Modern appearance, rose of Rose that usually has high-pointed buds and smooth foliage, similar to a Hybrid Tea Rose.

Mutation See Sport.

Old appearance, rose of Rose with bloom of cupped or rosette shape, rather than the pointed bud and informal flower of a Modern Rose; the plant usually having rough textured leaves, i.e. Gallica, Centifolia, etc.

Organic fertilizer A fertilizer made from natural materials rather than chemicals.

Patent appellation The variety denomination which is protected by Plant Breeders' Rights worldwide. For David Austin varieties it is prefixed with Aus eg Ausmas Graham Thomas.

Perpetual flowering A rose that continues to flower in the same year after the first flush of bloom, though not necessarily continually.

Pistil Female organ of a flower consisting of the stigma, style and ovary.

Pollen parent The male parent of a variety.

Pompon A small rounded bloom with regular short petals.

Quartered A flower in which the centre petals are folded into four.

Quilled petals Petals folded in the form of a quill.

Rambler-like I use this term to describe roses bearing large sprays of small blooms similar to those of a small-flowered Rambling Rose, particularly a Multiflora Rambler.

Recessive gene A gene that is dominated by another, rendering it ineffective unless two copies of the gene are present.

Recurrent flowering See Perpetual flowering.

Remontant See Perpetual flowering.

Repeat flowering See Perpetual flowering.

Roots, roses on their own Not budded on to a stock; grown from cuttings.

Root stock The host plant on to which a cultivated variety is budded.

Rugose Leaves with a rough, wrinkled surface. Hence the Rugosa roses.

Scion A shoot or bud used for grafting on to a root stock.

Seedling A rose grown from seed. In the context of this book, the offspring of two specific varieties.

Sepal One of the five green divisions of the calyx.

Shrub A rose that is normally pruned lightly and allowed to grow in a more natural form, as opposed to a bush which is pruned close to the ground.

Species A wild rose.

Sport A change in the genetic make up of the plant, as for example when a pink rose suddenly produces a white flower eg Mary Rose and Winchester Cathedral.

Spreading shrub A shrub on which the branches tend to extend outwards rather than vertically.

Stamen The male organ of a flower, consisting of the filament and anther, which produces pollen.

Stigma The end of the pistil or female flower organ.

Stock See Root-stock

Style The stem of the pistil which joins the stigma to the ovary.

Sucker A shoot growing from the root stock instead of from the budded variety.

Tetraploid A plant with four sets of chromosomes.

Trade designation See Denomination.

Triploid A plant with three sets of chromosomes. It usually grows well but is sterile.

Upright shrub A rose in which the growth tends to be vertical.

Variety Strictly speaking, a naturally occurring variation of a species. The popular meaning, so far as roses are concerned, is a distinct type of cultivated rose.

× Indicates a hybrid

181

Bibliography

American Rose Society's *Annuals*, from 1917.

Austin, David *The English Roses*, Conran Octopus, 2005.

Bean, W.J., *Trees and Shrubs Hardy in the British Isles*, Murray, 8th edn. revised.

Bois, Eric and Trechslin, Anne-Marie, *Roses*, 1962.

Bunyard, A.E., *Old Garden Roses*, Collingridge, 1936.

Dobson, B.R., *Combined Rose List. Hard to Find Roses and Where to Find Them*, Beverly R. Dobson, Irvington, New York 10533, 1985.

Edwards, G., *Wild and Old Garden Roses*, David & Charles, Newton Abbot, 1975; Hafner, New York, 1975.

Ellwanger, H.B., *The Rose*, Dodd-Mead, New York, 1822; 1914.

Fisher, John, *The Companion to Roses*, Viking, 1986

Fletcher, H.L.V., *The Rose Anthology*, Newnes, 1963.

Foster-Melliar, Rev. A., *The Book of the Rose*, Macmillan, 1894; 1910.

Gault S.M. and Synge P.M., *The Dictionary of Roses in Colour*, Michael Joseph and Ebury Press, 1970.

Gore, C.F., *The Book of Roses or The Rose Fancier's Manual*, 1838; Heyden, 1978.

Griffiths, Trevor, *The Book of Old Roses*, Michael Joseph, 1984.

Griffiths, Trevor, *The Book of Classic Old Roses*, Michael Joseph, 1986.

Harkness, Jack, *Roses*, Dent, 1978.

Hillier Manual of Trees and Shrubs, *The*, 3rd rev edn, David & Charles 2007.

Hole, S. Reynolds, *A Book about Roses*, William Blackwood, 1896.

Hollis, L., *Roses*, Collingridge, 1969; 2nd edn. with new illustrations, 1974.

Jekyll, G. and Mawley, E., *Roses for English Gardens*, Country Life, 1902; reprinted by Antique Collectors' Club, Woodbridge, 1982.

Keays, F.L., *Old Roses*, Macmillan, New York, 1935; facsimile edn. Heyden, Philadelphia and London, 1978.

Kordes, Wilhelm, *Roses*, Studio Vista, 1964.

Krussman, G., *Roses*, English edn, Batsford, 1982.

Lawrence, Mary, *A Collection of Roses* from Nature, 1799.

Le Grice, E.B., *Rose Growing Complete*, Faber & Faber, 1965.

Lord, Tony, *Designing with Roses*, Frances Lincoln, 1999.

McFarland, J.H., *Modern Roses*, 8th edn, McFarland Co., USA, 1980.

McFarland, J.H., *Roses of the World in Colour*, Cassell, 1936.

Mansfield, T.C., *Roses in Colour and Cultivation*, Collins, 1947.

Nottle, T., *Growing Old Fashioned Roses in Australia and New Zealand*, Kangaroo Press, 1983.

Olson, Jerry and John Whitman, *Growing Roses in Cold Climates*, Contemporary Books, 1998.

Paul, William, *The Rose Garden*, 10th edn, Simpkin, Marshall, Hamilton, Kent & Co., 1903.

Pemberton, Rev. J.H., *Roses, Their History, Development and Cultivation*, Longmans Green 1908; rev. edn. 1920.

Phillips, Roger and Rix, Martyn, *The Ultimate Guide to Roses*, Macmillan, 2004.

Quest-Ritson, Charles and Brigid, *The Royal Horticultural Society Encyclopaedia of Roses*, Dorling Kindersely, 2005.

Redouté, P.J., *Les Roses*, 1817–24, reprinted by Taschen, 2001.

RHS Plantfinder 2007–2008, Dorling Kindersely, 2007.

Ridge, A., *For the Love of a Rose*, Faber & Faber, 1965.

Rivers, T., *The Rose Amateur's Guide*, Longmans Green, 1837.

Ross, D., *Shrub Roses in Australia*, Deane Ross, 1981.

Royal National Rose Society's *Annuals*, from 1911.

Shepherd, R., *History of the Rose*, Macmillan, New York, 1966.

Steen, N., *The Charm of Old Roses*, Herbert Jenkins, 1966.

Thomas, G.S., *The Old Shrub Roses*, Phoenix House, 1955.

Thomas, G.S., *Shrub Roses of Today*, Phoenix House, 1962.

Thomas, G.S., *Climbing Roses Old and New*, Phoenix House, 1965.

Thompson, Richard, *Old Roses for Modern Gardens*, Van Nostrand, New York, 1959.

Warner, C., *Climbing Roses*, Tiptree Books.

Willmott, Ellen, *The Genus Rosa*, Murray, issued in parts 1910–14.

Young, Norman, *The Complete Rosarian*, Hodder & Stoughton, 1971.

Index
Figures in italics indicate an illustration